PUBLIC SPEAKING

Overcoming Fear of Public Speaking and Improve Your Leadership With Better Conversation

(Master Persuasion Skills for Better Engagements)

Chris Abrahams

Published by Rob Miles

© Chris Abrahams

All Rights Reserved

Communication Skills: Overcoming Fear of Public Speaking and Improve Your Leadership With Better Conversation (Master Persuasion Skills for Better Engagements)

ISBN 978-1-989990-00-1

All rights reserved. No part of this guide may be reproduced in any form without permission in writing from the publisher except in the case of brief quotations embodied in critical articles or reviews.

Legal & Disclaimer

The information contained in this book is not designed to replace or take the place of any form of medicine or professional medical advice. The information in this book has been provided for educational and entertainment purposes only.

The information contained in this book has been compiled from sources deemed reliable, and it is accurate to the best of the Author's knowledge; however, the Author cannot guarantee its accuracy and validity and cannot be held liable for any errors or omissions. Changes are periodically made to this book. You must consult your doctor or get professional medical advice before using any of the suggested remedies, techniques, or information in this book.

Upon using the information contained in this book, you agree to hold harmless the Author from and against any damages, costs, and expenses, including any legal fees potentially resulting from the application of any of the information provided by this guide. This disclaimer applies to any damages or injury caused by the use and application, whether directly or indirectly, of any advice or information presented, whether for breach of contract, tort, negligence, personal injury, criminal intent, or under any other cause of action.

You agree to accept all risks of using the information presented inside this book. You need to consult a professional medical practitioner in order to ensure you are both able and healthy enough to participate in this program.

Table of Contents

INTRODUCTION 1

CHAPTER 1: LEXICAL SPEECH CULTURE 3

CHAPTER 2: WHY WE FOREVER HOLD OUR PEACE 14

CHAPTER 3: WHAT YOU NEED TO OVERCOME YOUR FEAR AND BELIEVE IN YOURSELF 26

CHAPTER 4: HOW TO PRACTICE YOUR SPEECH 37

CHAPTER 5: RESONATION 44

CHAPTER 6: OVERCOMING A LIFETIME OF STAGE FRIGHT 49

CHAPTER 7: ASKING HIM OR HER FOR A DATE 63

CHAPTER 8: PURPOSE, IMPORTANCE, AND PRINCIPLES OF COMMUNICATION 67

CHAPTER 9: NETWORKING EFFECTIVELY THROUGH COMMUNICATION 77

CHAPTER 10: PREPARE TO FIGHT 82

CHAPTER 11: STRUCTURE OF THIS WORK: CLEARING THE PAST, PRESENT AND FUTURE 87

CHAPTER 12: ENGAGING YOUR AUDIENCE 89

CHAPTER 13: SPEECH BODY 94

CHAPTER 14: DO YOUR HOMEWORK. THEN DO THE EXTRA CREDIT. 111

CHAPTER 15: SPEAK ABOUT WHAT YOU KNOW 117

CHAPTER 16: EFFECTIVE INTRODUCTION 122

CHAPTER 17: THE THREE VERY BEST PLACES WHERE THE BEST TOPICS ARE EASY TO FIND 132

CHAPTER 18: THE FAR EASIER AND BETTER WAY TO PREPARE YOUR TALK 146

CHAPTER 19: HOW TO CONTROL THE AUDIENCE INTERACTION 154

CHAPTER 20: 3 STEPS TO BECOMING THE MOST CHARISMATIC PERSON IN THE ROOM 171

CHAPTER 21: THE INTERVIEW PLAN 175

CHAPTER 22: THE POWER OF CHARM 183

CHAPTER 23: SELF CONFIDENCE: THE FOUNDATION OF PROFESSIONAL SPEAKERS 186

CONCLUSION 192

Introduction

Most people have a fear of public speaking but with the help of this book you can learn how to give great speeches and unleash your potential in doing presentations. Public speaking is listed as the greatest fear of man. The thought of delivering a speech to a crowd of unfamiliar faces delivers a kind of anxiety that if not conquered, will lead to a greater disaster.

Trembling and mumbling in front of a big audience is embarrassing and will break your self-esteem. You may lose big opportunities or mess up special events if you let this fear overpower your skills.

This book will give you effective tips on how to deliver a speech that will leave a fascinated audience that gives eager acceptance to your message. Once you learn what there is to public speaking, you really will wonder what it was that you were worried about. You will be able to deliver that speech with great authority and power so that it will be well received by everyone.

Chapter 1: Lexical Speech Culture

ntelligence - an innate ability to think, is in every mentally healthy person. And each strong speaker is distinguished by the ability to think publicly. His thought can be born in the presence of a large number of people anc be immediately stated by him. In this regard, the speaker must be fluent in the vocabulary and rules of the language he speaks. This helps him to most accurately express his thought and choose the most vivid words corresponding in meaning to the phenomenon or action that he describes. The speaker needs to constantly work on himself, improving his speech. And to know that in a public statement it is important to:

Use words correctly

Use slang, dialect and vernacular words only if justified

Apply stable phrases

Avoid mistakes in the pronunciation of words

Correctly put the stress on some words

From several synonyms choose the word that is most suitable for the style of utterance

Delimit paronyms ("graduate" - "diploma")

Accurately and moderately use a foreign language, archaic words, and terms

Decrypt abbreviations;

Precisely and know where to use phraseological turns

Delete "word-parasites."

The ability to choose the right synonym helps to more accurately reflect the tint of the displayed phenomenon or action. For example, falling can also be done in different ways: to tumble, to fall down, to plow, to plop, flop, smack, topple.

Speak - to express oneself, to express oneself, to rant, to go broke, oratory, to spill nightingale, to pronounce, utter, broadcast, casually drop.

Rain happens: drizzle, heavy rain, torrential, strong, shallow, sparse, oblique, mushroom, and it pours, lashes, drizzles, drips, pours like a bucket.

Dictionaries should become the speaker's handbooks, and public speakers must have their own because they will be needed for their work all the time.

About words and phrase-parasites - a separate conversation, because they "infect" the speech of many people. They are harmful in that they negatively affect the brevity, expressiveness, correctness, and accuracy of speech and take away its strength and emotionality. Some manage to insert "so to speak," "here," "so," "this is the most," "understand," "mean," "that is," "well, you understand," "and I am like that," "like would," "that," "began to be," "well," "generally," "well, yes," "eh"... in every sentence. And even a few in one phrase ("I want, so to speak, to explain to you something ...").

The reason for clogging speech with parasites is simple - a person does not have enough energy to concentrate on conveying his thoughts to the listener. And in order to gain strength for a new phrase, he inserts a word - a parasite, receiving a kind of pause. People with weak energy of thought, when they need to speak out, pronounce instead of the normal words "well, yes," "that is," "generally," "e," "here."

It is clear that such a speech can neither convince nor captivate. Weedy words distract the listener's attention from the meaning of what was said and cause confidence that the speaker is boring, insecure, and uninteresting. Therefore, you need to control your speech and abandon the words of the parasites.

How it's done? First, we make sure that the parasite words are in our speech. For this, we simply record our speech on the recorder in different communication situations: with friends, in a company, at a meeting or meeting, etc. Then we listen.

Emphasis: listening to yourself at first will be disgusting; here, you need to overcome the feeling of rejection. But - there were no people in the world who, from the very beginning, from the first listening, as their own speech, and we are not an exception. It happens that for the first time having heard his speech from the side, a person experiences great dissatisfaction with himself.

Listening, we study speech for parasitic words, write down which of them "sin," and then get rid of it. We introduce the habit of constantly controlling our speech. The reception is this: we speak under control - you speak yourself and then immediately listen to yourself - what you say. And do it everywhere!

At first, it will not be easy to keep attention in two directions; then, the habit will develop. You need to pay attention to the moment when the word - the parasite will be ready to fly off the tongue and just stop it, with an effort of will, even if it takes a short pause. Then continue to speak, carefully choosing words, and polishing the spoken phrases. If you follow the words like parasites for 21 days, then the habit of pronouncing them will disappear. If you follow the speech for two months, then the ability to speak without parasites will take root, but then from time to time, you need to listen to yourself from the side so as not to return to the past. Control over your speech needs to be brought into your habits. Thanks to this, you can learn to speak weightily, briefly, and competently.

To help in the fight against parasites, you can call friends, relatives, and colleagues. Having explained their problem to them, ask them to draw your attention to the moments when these words are heard in a speech. To make the process more efficient, you can involve other people in it and introduce a rule - for each spoken word - the parasite makes a monetary penalty in the general piggy bank. This technique very well helps to cope with the problem.

Emphasis: suppose that you have already rid your speech of parasites and are completely without them. But, suddenly, they again begin to fly off the tongue - this happens, and this is an alarming bell. He says that the strength of a person is weakening; he is becoming more insecure. The reason to look for in a psychological state, perhaps stress, prolonged stress affects the level of strength. Do not delay - go to a psychologist for help or apply self-correction methods.

Now about how vocabulary affects success. Man is what words he pronounces. Our well-being, financial success, career growth, love of loved ones, respect of others, relationships at work, and with the opposite sex, it all depends on what words we use in our speech. And the more a person speaks the word, the more he speaks correctly and positively, the more he is successful and realizes his plans faster.

When teaching journalists the ethics of the profession, much attention is paid to the responsibility for the words used. About forty years ago, this responsibility was considered only from a moral point of view. However, there is another facet in this topic that many people are not aware of. The fact is that the words we write, pronounce (mentally or aloud) have energy and vibration: positive, neutral, and negative. In a word, you can either improve or make life worse. Recall the proverb: "Call a man a pig three times, he grunts."

Today, scientists have already proved that it is on knowledge of the energy power and vibration of the word that conspiracies of healers and witches are based, as well as slander. That kind of positive words greatly improves health. The speaker needs to use words that create a life-affirming attitude - this is the key to professional success.

Lexical syllogisms do not make a good impression. For example, in speeches, it often sounds: "I want to say," "I want to wish," "I would like to." Hearing such a verbal conglomeration, you feel the urge to make an amendment: "if you want to say - say it," "if you want to congratulate - congratulate," "I would like to - take it off" and just want it." How do these phrases work? The dynamic words "congratulate," "wish," are delayed by the inert "I want to," and, as a result, the said phrase has no effect. The dynamic "want" is replaced by "wanted," stumbling over the uncertainty of "would." Such combinations do double harm.

Firstly, they make the idea vague, preventing the listener from concentrating on it. Secondly, they cause a feeling that the speaker is unsure of himself and what he is saying. Compare the above phrases with new, more energetic, more specific: "I will say," "I want to." They evoke a feeling that you are a strong, self-confident person, who knows their goals and objectives, pronounces them.

Now let's talk about sounds. Each of them also carries its own energy and vibration and, combined into a word, they give a certain effect. What words we say is very important. The way we allow ourselves to be called is also. Therefore, if there is a desire to deploy the program of your life and quickly realize your goals, call yourself a full name. And watch the changes begin to take place. It seems important to present yourself in full name. Short names, as well as nicknames, are excluded for successful people. They come from the inability to use the energy of their names.

If possible, find information on how Napoleon Bonaparte signed in different periods of his life. And if you carefully analyze the signatures and relate them to the life events of this person, you can make some discoveries for yourself. We will not disclose our observations now, let this be the reader's homework.

Dear speakers! When using words, be careful. The word can really kill, if not morally, then energetically. The word can belittle and may exalt. Therefore, for your own good, success, and prosperity, use good words that carry positive energy. Use them in public speaking, because people respond to them faster. "A good word is also pleasant for a cat," and even more so for a person.

Well, and it will come back a hundredfold to you because oratory has a great driving force. According to Cicero, in republican Rome, a person who owns a word was looked upon as a god.

Chapter 2: Why We Forever Hold our Peace

When you hear someone say that they would rather die than speak in public, don't take them lightly because they may not be joking at all. Fear of public speaking is a serious issue and it's among with the top fears, along with fear of death, flying, and spiders.

Marked by stomach cramps, pounding heart, shaky hands, dry mouth, quivering voice, and cold sweaty palms, fear of public speaking is shared by millions of people worldwide and is rooted in social phobia. We fear being judged and evaluated by other people. It may be a psychological response to the thought of other people thinking of you in a certain manner, but it has a physical translation. Public speaking, aside from being considered a psychological threat, becomes a physical one too, and since the body can't differentiate between a psychological and physical one, we react as if a tiger is ready to bite our heads off.

Feeling strong emotions such as fear and anxiety places stress on you and triggers the fight-or-flight response. Needed hormones flood and course through your body and are responsible for increasing your heart rate, tightening your muscles, hastening your breathing, etc. Hands down, these bodily reactions are useful when you are against a wild animal in the savannah. They will help you escape danger. However, it says a lot about you if you escape from your audience and leave your speaking engagement. At the end of the day, the physical responses instigated by our body systems do not really fit the situation so we have to find ways to calm ourselves down and make our body and mind realize that we're not facing extinction when we take those first steps towards the stage.

To start, let's debunk some myths that other people say are sure ways to overcoming the pterodactyls in your stomach when you are about to speak.

Always tell a joke to start your speech with a bang

No. The art of telling jokes is a minefield that you must tread with care. They're actually difficult to deliver because you have to keep in mind their content and timing. Trust me, you will want the floor to open up and eat you if you have to stand there like an idiot and wait for somebody to laugh at your joke. Moreover, humor can easily be offensive and inappropriate because culture plays a very big part in its success. This is just one of the reasons that explains why it's not a good idea to begin a speech with a joke. Particularly for rookie speakers, it's an additional pressure on your part and the unpredictability of it can make everything go downhill. However, if you are really adamant about using a joke, it would be safer to navigate it so that the joke is on you and not on other people.

Also, don't wait for other people to laugh; just continue with what you intend to say. If people understand and catch your joke, then it's well and good. If they didn't, continuing without pausing will provide you the chance to escape the embarrassment.

One mistake equals one prayer for your death

It's not the end of your speech—or of the world—if you commit a blunder while you are speaking. Making them isn't as important as learning how to recover and learn from them.

Memorize your speech word by word

This will overload your mind with the thousands of words that you have to remember and will worsen your anxiety as you pressure yourself to remember all those details. Instead of committing to memory every letter, remember the main points and sub-points of your speech. The tendency with memorization is, if your mind goes blank in the middle of the speech, you have to start all over again to find your bearing. Furthermore, it can be quite obvious when you are just speaking memorized words as your speech will come off as robotic, canned, and too polished.

Your listeners are your arch enemies

This can't always be applied to everyone because, let's face it, there are just people who live for other people's misery; but normally, the audience is not there to criticize you or bring you down. Most of face-to-face audiences will empathize with the emotional state of the speaker and are there for the content of the message and not for the chance to have the last laugh of the day.

Public speaking is an inborn talent

It's true that there are people who will find it less demanding to speak in public than others. However, the majority of brilliant speakers out there weren't excellent at speeches the moment they opened their mouths at age 3. It takes experience, hard work, and practice to deliver a speech with the ease that you expect. If you think you suck at speaking right now, don't lose hope because there's still a great chance of getting better at it.

Fearing public speaking must mean you are not good at it

No one gets a pass from the rush of adrenaline that comes hand-in-hand with delivering a presentation in front of a crowd. You know the difference between successful speakers and newbies? It's that successful speakers have learned why they should and how to transform and use fear to their advantage.

Fear and stress won't stay the ultimate villains in every situation there is. Stress can actually be helpful for one's development. Psychology reveals that a modicum of stress is needed to learn and perform well. Fear, in the case of public speaking can actually boost the quality of our performance since it gets the systems of our body working. Our awareness heightens, and fear can improve our concentration as well as sharpen our thinking. Did you ever notice how people who are working under fear achieve some impossible feats–things that they usually can't when their emotions are positive or neutral? When his place is on fire, a person can lift a huge refrigerator all by himself. That's what stress does to you. It makes you more equipped to battle through whatever predicament you are in.

Of course, we're talking about moderate amounts of stress and fear. It should be obvious that too much stress can stop us from doing well. Therefore, we need to take some measures to reduce our apprehension when it comes to speaking by first exposing ourselves to the experience. Unfortunately, nowadays, opportunities for speaking in public have been curtailed by the advancement in technology. With the advent of online and social media, our communication skills are not getting brushed up enough. Instead of doing personal conversations, we type our thoughts and hit enter to send our opinions across.

Even at work, communication amongst employees is mostly not in the oral and verbal form anymore.

Everything boils down to a lack of experience in public speaking. Don't fret, because there are a lot of things you can do to reduce—and perhaps totally overcome—your fear of public speaking.

Think positively

Be optimistic about the idea of speaking. Thinking of only the negative things that may happen won't benefit you in general. Focusing on your failure would also cripple you from pushing through.

Visualize

Visualization involves thinking through the steps of a certain activity in your mind. You mentally walk through the sequence of events and use your imagination to create a scenario of success. Achievers practice visualization to build up a positive attitude around achieving their goals. Athletes imagine reaching that finish line or dunking that ball while business executives think of sealing that multi-million deal.

Basically, what you have to do is think of a goal that you want to achieve. Let's say that you badly need to deliver a business presentation that you've been working on for the past few months in front of an audience composed of the high-level administrators in your company. You mentally picture yourself entering the board room, standing in front of the room, starting with your introduction, proceeding to the body of your speech, incorporating visual aids, and giving a brilliant end to your speech. Think about how the people in front of you would nod in appreciation, how maybe one or two would give you a round of applause, and how some of them would crack a smile at the quality of your delivery. Focusing on the positive outcome that you envision will relax your body and mind and they will respond to the image as if it were real.

However, you must note that visualization isn't enough. Just because you spent hours visualizing doesn't mean you can slack off in preparing and practicing for your speech. Paired with the mental work is a corresponding physical effort that must be observed. A basketball player, of course, can't just keep on visualizing about those points. He must also sweat blood and tears in the process to hone his skills.

Relax

Before entering what you think is the room of doom, engage in your choice of relaxation techniques. You can opt to meditate before it's time to speak. Free your mind of the distracting and off-putting thoughts swirling around inside that head of yours.

Some may also find it effective to get a massage in order to help their bodies release the accumulated tension from all the preparation done for the event. Try the activities that would normally relax you. Read, drink your favorite beverage, or find comfort in your most preferred food.

Another effective technique would also be to breathe deeply. Whenever you feel like your breaths are chasing each other, become aware of how the air is going into your lungs and out of your nose as you deeply inhale and exhale.

Focusing on facts, not fears

Don't dwell on irrational thoughts that might not even come true. I will bore my audience. I will stammer in the middle of my sentences. Oh no, my mind will go blank! Mull over the positive facts that you can think of. Remember that you prepared well for the event. Remember that you did all you could do to make your speech worthy of being heard.

Don't expect perfection

No perfect speech exists in the history of speeches. Even those you think are faultless have some errors somewhere along the line. The additional stress that people feel about talking is adhering to the misconception that everything should be perfect in order for the audience to appreciate the speech. It isn't actually like that. Your listeners can still commend you for a job well done even with a stutter or two during your delivery.

Don't get disappointed in yourself if you find that you've lost your place as you speak. Just calmly reverse the order of your statements and be flexible when it comes to the content of your speech. Your audience doesn't know what you are planning to say so it won't notice if you've skipped a point or two.

Reduce anxiety by preparing well

By far, this is one of the most effective methods of overcoming your anxiety. Be prepared for your speech and know that whatever may be thrown your way, you will be able to handle it.

Chapter 3: What You Need To Overcome Your Fear and Believe In Yourself

---

Why do some people have a hard time speaking in front of others?

Some of the more common reasons include:

Fear of facing an audience

Scared of Q&As

Fear English isn't good

Anxiety about confidence

Afraid of faltering

No idea about the topic

Afraid of drawing a blank while talking

Afraid to look right at the audience

What is the fear of public speaking? It's known as Glossophobia, and millions of people suffer from it. There are all kinds of reasons people are fearful of speaking in public, hindering them from effective speech communications. And, there is just as much advice about speech communication as there are reasons for the fear. What are some helpful tips to keep in mind to move past your speech anxiety?

You Cannot Always Be Fearless

Fear is considered the most important hindrance when it comes to public speaking. Fear is a part of your mindset. If you believe you are worried and anxious about something, the reality is that you are.

If you think you're not, then you're not. Fear is always waiting in the wings; waiting to show itself. You must remain calm to move past that fear.

Find Your Authority and Your Voice

When speaking about a topic, it's important to know what you're talking about. Be sure the topic you choose is something you have a passion for, completely understand and can take questions on.

Never try passing off a subject you have little knowledge on because, in most cases, you will fail and the audience will see right through you.

Luck is not the essence of success, not when it comes to public speaking. Passion is what you need to convince audiences that you have an authority of the topic you are speaking about.

Be Competent In Your Abilities

If you're going to talk in front of an audience, make sure you are competent enough to do so. Competency is a must-have skill for public speaking.

You can gain competency by signing up for a speech training class and being an active member. You should also have plenty of experience on the topic you'll be discussing.

Be Truthful When Speaking

According to an old saying, if you have any doubt, speak the truth. Why is that? It's much easier to tell the truth than have to remember a lie. Also, if you change your story too often, people will immediately catch on. When you tell people the truth, they feel can feel your energy level rise. Your face will light up, and you'll feel excited about what you're talking about.

Your fear of public speaking is not going to go away overnight. However, it can happen, if you can remember the four tips listed above.

You can always maintain success in public speaking if you can remember to be passionate about your subject, feel confident in your subject and yourself and speak the truth all the time.

Is it possible to become a successful public speaker? Absolutely! Just remember not to lie and be excited about what you have to say.

Perceived Failure Is What Causes Public Speaking Fear

Public speaking skills are like any skills — the more success you have with them, the more confident you become in yourself. Thus, the more public speaking you do, the more confident you can be with your skills.

The same goes true for perceived failures. The more you feel you've failed; the scarier public speaking is likely to be.

It's normal to feel anxious or nervous when talking in front of people. However, the fear of public speaking doesn't have to follow you for the rest of your life.

Where Does The Fear Of Public Speaking Originate?

Think about the kinds of skills you have acquired in your lifetime. You didn't always know how to ride a book, play a musical instrument, sing, drive a car or work your smartphone.

It took time to master these skills, and until you did, you may have been nervous about it.

This is normal!

It takes time to gain confidence in yourself to master these skills. The same goes true for public speaking. When you gain confidence in your ability to do a certain skill, it becomes second nature. It becomes easier to do the more times you have to do something.

In the beginning, you are going to fail — that much is certain. However, your failures will ultimately lead to success so long as you learn from them and use them to your benefit.

Also, the more successes you have, the more confidence you have in what you are doing.

Don't think so?

Go back to the driving analogy. When you get behind the wheel by yourself for the first time, you may be worried about what could happen.

Chances are, your first experience isn't going to go right. You may back into a pole or you hit a parked vehicle. It's the fear that stops you from moving forward, but you know you have to keep going to be successful.

The same is true for public speaking!

You may be afraid to do something, but if you don't try, the fear is always going to be there, and you'll never move past it.

Success Leads To Your Skills In Public Speaking

A key way to learn a skill is to begin with a task that has no real risks behind it. For instance, a child learns driving a car on an empty road or parking lot usually with a coach or parent.

Once the child has an increased confidence level, they may start making right-hand or left-hand turns around the neighborhood. And, as the confidence grows even more, they may start driving in traffic – something slow than onto busier streets.

The last thing they aim for is the interstate.

If your goal is to speak in public, you need to start with the same premise as the driving one. Slow at first, building up the confidence until it's finally there!

For public speaking, begin slowly. The first step is to speak up at a staff meeting. The majority of executives and managers want to hear ideas or issues during these meetings. Be sure to talk at least one time during them.

Once you've gained confidence here, take it to the next step by volunteering to do a report during the staff meeting. If you're confident in doing these, try something a little riskier such as asking questions of the audience in a big presentation.

You're going to be nervous. This is known as public speaking fear. However, the more complex the presentations you do, the more confidence you have in yourself and the easier these presentations become. Before you know, it's second nature.

How A Public Speaking Coach Can Help You Garner Confidence In Yourself

Similar to the coach or parent who taught you how to drive, a coach for public speaking can help you overcome your fear. For example, going to a parking lot to learn how to drive means learning how to park correctly.

This may have taken some time, but the hard part is the lack of frame of reference you had to compare that skill. You'll always question yourself if you're doing the right thing or not. This is nervousness.

A coach will tell you if you're doing something right or wrong.

Now, there's no reason you have to seek out a professional public speaking coach. All you have to do is find someone you have a good rapport with and has great public speaking skills and see if they'll be willing to critique you and offer you some constructive criticism.

If time is of the essence, you may want to seek out a professional coach. This person can assist you in developing these skills in a couple of days that most people take years to learn and master. They can also help you to move past bad habits (fidgeting, nail biting, etc.).

For example, I wanted to play golf in my 20s. I didn't have a lot of money, so I purchased used golf clubs and practiced on the city golf course. I got good, but still had issues with my slice.

When groups of friends and I played, I always seemed to lack in points. Since I thought I wasn't any good for golfing, I quit playing.

It was years later when I tried to start playing again. I asked a golf professional for some help to get competitive. He said it was going to take longer to learn because I was standing wrong for so long.

It was going to take time for me to correct the stance and change things around. I was used to the swing, and learning a new habit meant unlearning what I was used to.

Simply put, if I had gotten feedback early on, I would have saved a lot of aggravation and time. The same holds true for public speaking. Be sure to find someone who has overcome their fear and allow them to coach you. This person can assist you in quickly eliminating the fear.

Chapter 4: How to Practice Your Speech

Practicing your speech is essential to having a good speech, but practice is not going to make your speech perfect. What will make it perfect is revising and learning from your practices at home with or without an audience. There are many way you can practice a speech when you're at home, but let's first discuss what practicing is going to do for you.

So why should you practice a speech?

Practicing a speech is not going to make you perfect in any sense, but it is going to point out some things to you that will make your speech better.

- You'll be able to hear awkward expressions and tongue-twisters you may not have seen when you were writing and editing. Speaking the words out loud exposes those flaws, unlike reading or writing.

- You can gauge your energy level and adjust it so you're fired up in certain parts and a little more subdued in others. You can also determine if you're bored with the speech, which will definitely bore your audience.

- You can gauge your timing. Once you're experienced, you'll learn how many words are going to fit into a ten-minute time slot. Until then, you have to practice a complete speech to know if you're going to be under or over your time slot.

- Rehearsing is going to reduce your nervousness and improve your confidence in your material.

So how do you rehearse a speech at home?

Rehearsing just one time is going to improve your confidence in the speech you've written. You can practice for sixty hours or sixty minutes, but either way you should use some of these tips to make your speech the best it can be.

Recreate the Setting

Reading the speech at a computer screen is not going to make you feel more confident about your material. That is unless you're going to be doing a webcast. If that's the case, practice at the screen all you want! Otherwise, try to duplicate your setting like this:

- If you can book the room you'll be speaking in, then go for it and practice there! That's the best place to practice because you'll be able to hear yourself talking and hear your pitch, speed, and know how much room you have for gesturing.

- Stand up so you can hear your voice being projected. This gives you confidence and will tell you when to speak up or tone it down.

- Rehearse with your props and visual aids so you know where they're going to go after you're done with them. No one wants to trip over a visual aid while they're talking.

- Practice with an audience you know will give you feedback.

- Consider what you're going to wear. Will it create complications or will it inhibit your gestures? Make sure it's comfortable and you'll feel professional in it!

- Take notes as you practice so you know where to improve the second time you practice.

- Don't hesitate to stop in the middle of rehearsal and jot down some ideas. Capture those internal emotions immediately and figure out how you can express them to the audience or deal with them if it's stage fright.

Experiment

Don't be afraid to try out different gestures, voices, and staging. This is imperative for your introduction, conclusion, and key points throughout the speech.

Timing

Most speeches have to be delivered in a certain amount of time, so use a stopwatch or an app on your phone to time your speech and make sure it's within the amount you need.

Get Feedback

After the rehearsal, you want to actively ask members of the audience for some feedback. Did your humor get any laughs? Did you keep their attention throughout the speech? If you can't answer those questions, ask the audience. You can also ask them other things, such as:

- What was your favorite part and why?

- What would you want to see improved?

- How can the speech be improved for the next time?

This is much better than just asking if they liked it. It gives them the opportunity to be truly honest with you.

Use Audio Recordings

It might seem silly, but audio recordings of your speech are going to tell you your pace, pause, and pitch when you're delivering the speech. Assess phrases that sound good and ones that are awkward. Listen for any filler words like um and ah and notice if you stumble. Time the speech and individual components of the speech when you listen to it.

Video Recordings

A video recording is a very powerful tool. All your movements and habits are captured on film and you get to study them so you can change what you're doing on stage. You can look to see if:

- Your gestures work.

- The gestures are synchronized with words.

- The gestures are varied or all the same.

- Whether or not you're smiling.

- If you're fidgeting or using distracting motions.

- If you're swaying from nervousness.

Practicing at home with just a mirror is suitable, too because it will allow you to see what you're doing and let you hear yourself. Just remember to practice. Even just once can change your entire speech!

Chapter 5: Resonation

Resonation plays an important role in giving you the confidence to speak freely and approach someone more authoritatively.

What is Resonance?

Resonance refers to the amplification of sound. It is meant to adjust the timbre of your voice by stressing on specific vocal qualities over others. To put it simply, resonators help to make tone quality better by brightening and warming them up. It increases the volume and the start sound. It is like a recital hall where people sitting in all corners can clearly hear the voice of the singer singing on the stage.

It is important to create a well resonating voice so that everybody can hear it and you have good control over it.

Where does Vocal Resonance Occur?

Resonance occurs in the pharyngeal cavity and is a part of the nasal cavities, throat, mouth and larynx. The names for these areas are known as laryngopharynx, oropharynx, and nasopharynx.

Although there are other cavity resonators in the body that help to create vocal sounds, they are usually not considered to be easy to control. For example, the trachea can produce a grunting sound, but cannot be controlled. Lungs and bronchi make vibrations and so do the laryngeal cavities. These reflect the sound, vibrate and resonate like sounding boards. Essentially speaking, everything that lies in between the head and the chest tend to enhance vocal resonance. Even singers do not have a control over the resonators but can feel the vibrations.

What is Laryngopharynx Resonance?

The laryngopharynx is a part of the throat and lies between the top of the larynx and the bottom of the tongue and adds warmth to the voice. This area has muscles and tubes around it. Singers have the capability of switching up the diameter and the length of the laryngopharynx, but not its shape. Having a higher larynx can shorten the tube and a lower larynx can lengthen it. One that lies in between is best for singers with the tube remaining four to five inches long. The diameter is usually large and disengages the muscles inside the tube.

Adding Warmth and Volume

If you happen to be someone whose voice is quite bright and would like to improve your tone, then you have to focus on laryngopharynx resonance, but do not over-stress it as it can lead to a sunken tone. The key is to enlarge the diameter of your throat by lowering the larynx and relaxing your throat. To do this, close your mouth and draw in a deep breath like you are about to yawn. You have to feel the larynx expand. You must adopt a neutral laryngeal pose that is not any higher than, or is slightly lower than, your usual speaking voice.

You have to stress on the "ah" while feeling the breath go deep just like you feel before yawning. If your resonance increases, then your volume and warmth will increase too.

What is Oropharynx Resonance?

The oropharynx happens to be the gap from the bottom of the tongue towards the soft palate. The mouth and the jawline, along with the lips, tend to determine this area's shape and size. When you lower the jaw, you tend to increase the gap, and when you close the jaw, you tend to decrease the gap. If you press the back of the tongue against the back of the mouth, then it produces a humming sound as it prevents air from going through the mouth. It is this very area where consonants are generated. Adjusting this area is what helps you speak but, if only this area is used while making a speech, it can be inconsistent and wonky.

Adding Brightness and Volume to Your Voice Using Nasopharynx Resonance

When it comes to adding brightness to your voice, it is important not to close off the space in the nasopharynx, especially while singing upscale. The best way to determine nasopharynx resonance is by pinching your nostrils while singing.

You will notice that some consonants are difficult and nearly impossible to sing, as they need larger amounts of air to move through the nostrils. These happen to be consonants such as "m" "n" and "ng." In case your voice happens to stress on these three consonants in particular, it means that you speak nasally. Instead, if there seem to be vibrations occurring in the bridge of your nose when you touch it, then you speak with a nasopharynx resonance.

Chapter 6: Overcoming A Lifetime Of Stage Fright

Stage fright, also referred to as performance anxiety is a persistent fear or phobia that crops up whenever you have to perform publicly. Often times, the fear of speaking or performing in front of people brews from anxiety issues. Mostly, this is due to low self-esteem and self-assurance, and the fear of being studied and judged.

If you experience stage fright, it is important to carry out effective stage fright treatment; doing so will help you overcome this problem. Overcoming performance anxiety is extremely important because until you get rid of your stage fright, you won't become an effective public speaker.

Although, public speaking may seem very cumbersome right now, it is not that difficult. With the help of this public speaking workbook, you can easily practice performance anxiety treatment to overcome this fear and be able to speak confidently in a conference or any social situation.

How To Overcome A Lifetime Of Performance Anxiety

To overcome a lifetime of performance anxiety:

Relax

To get rid of stage fright, the first thing you need to do is to relax. To the unexperienced or un-confident, public speaking brings with it confusion and fear; in this state, you are unable to realize that the fear is within.

You are the only one limiting yourself, the world, and those in it are not. To understand, and comprehend this notion, you must be in a calm state of mind. This is why it is essential to unwind. Diaphragmatic breathing and meditation are two excellent techniques for calming down your mind and understanding how your thoughts trick you into being fearful.

How to Do it

First, sit down comfortably and close your eyes. Now, focus on nothing but your breath, and draw in a deep breath. Fill your lungs with all the air it can hold and hold your breath for a count of five, count to five and slowly exhale. While you do that, concentrate on your breathing movements and nothing else. In about ten minutes, you will become calm and peaceful. Once you reach that state, you need to carry out the next step.

Study your thoughts

Take any negative thought and study it. Examine its behavior and observe what it does to your mind. For instance, we could analyze a thought such as "I cannot speak in front of people." Does this thought give you a good feeling or does it scare you? Keep studying it until you understand its true colors. Once you are able to grasp its evil nature, move to the next step.

Transform the Thought

After studying your thought, twist the nature of that thought and convert it into a slightly positive one. Delete the word 'cannot' from the thought and start chanting it. Observe how it makes you feel. Do you feel a slight surge of confidence building inside you? Yeah? Now brush up this thought a bit and add a confident tone to it. For instance, 'I speak confidently in front of people.' Now study what this thought does to your mind. Within minutes, you will understand the effect of a positive thought on your mind. This understanding will motivate you to thwart the thought for good.

Make many positive affirmations

Once you realize the power of positive thoughts, create many similar affirmations you can feed into your mind every now and then to help it overcome performance anxiety. Positive affirmations are healthy suggestions that convince your subconscious mind of your ability to do something. The more convinced your mind becomes, the easier it becomes for it to make you do something. If you convince your mind that you can face people and speak in front of them, it will actually help you become a confident public speaker.

For that, you need to continue injecting happy thoughts into it. Here are a few affirmations for you to overcome stage fright.

"I am the kind of person who finds it easy to face people."

"I am good at speaking in front of people."

"With every breath, I exhale my fears and inhale more confidence."

"I am an excellent public speaker."

"I release stress and phobias every moment and infuse more self-confidence in myself."

"I radiate confidence wherever I go."

"People are inspired by my self-assurance and public speaking skills."

"I speak easily in front of authority figures."

"I speak confidently on any topic at any time."

Feed these affirmations to your subconscious mind on a regular basis and soon, you will gain a newfound confidence that will kick out stage fright from your mind for good.

Start mingling with people

Once you start becoming confident, mingle with people more often. When you interact with people, you get the chance to communicate with them. This slowly reduces your fear of facing them. You understand that they are like you, which gives you the confidence to face them when you have to perform and develop public speaking skills.

See yourself as the authority figure

Quite often, you experience performance nervousness because you think, or find others to be superior to you. You feel that others are better than you are, or are at some sort of powerful position. This feeling intimidates you and extracts all the confidence in you. You become incompetent and unable to face them. If that's your case, you need to start visualizing yourself as the authority figure. You become nervous because you feel inferior to others. If you start feeling powerful and confident, you won't suffer from this complex issue anymore. You will understand that you are good enough and have what it takes to impress people. This helps you speak confidently. To gain that confidence, you can use a visualization technique.

Use your imagination or a mirror

Using a mirror or your imagination, start seeing yourself as a confident, a powerful person who makes eyes turn, and can impress anyone if given a chance. Once you envision that, observe how the new you behaves. Notice every move the mental you makes and start incorporating those details into your own self.

Start walking and talking in a similar manner, and within a little while, you will feel confident. By practicing this exercise for about 15 minutes every day, you will overcome stage fright because you will become more confident.

Start speaking in front of a small crowd

Once your fear starts diminishing, make a bold move. To complete your stage fright treatment, chose to put you 'new self' out there by speaking in front of a small crowd. Gather your friends somewhere and prepare a five-minute speech on any topic of your choice. Make sure you gather a supportive group.

Let them know your goal and then start speaking in front of them. You will become a little anxious but keep going, and speak for the full five minutes. By the time you finish, you will understand that it wasn't impossible. Difficult as it was, this was something you actually did. If you can face these people, you can face anybody.

Speak in front of an interactive crowd

Carry out the above practice at least twice a week until you become confident enough to face an interactive crowd and speak smoothly and confidently in front of them. Ask for more volunteers, preferably strangers and ask them to make that conference interactive for you. Interactive in this case means questions, suggestions, and ideas coming your way. Interactiveness will help you tackle different elements experienced in public speaking.

This practice will enhance your skill and help you become more confident. If you can communicate well when faced with various questions and suggestions, you have successfully managed your performance anxiety.

Make healthy lifestyle changes

Besides bringing positive changes to your personality, you as well need to bring healthy changes to your lifestyle. To bid farewell to stage fright for good, live healthy to feel, and be healthy.

Below are some lifestyle changes that will reduce performance anxiety and stage fright.

Limit your caffeine intake: A small cup of coffee a day is fine, but if your caffeine intake increases to more than 200mg per day, then things are bound to go wrong. An increased caffeine intake makes you jittery and can result in anxiety. Reduce your caffeine consumption and don't drink coffee at all when you have to speak publicly.

Drink citrus juice: Citrus juices are loaded with vitamins and minerals that make you feel fresh and energetic. In addition, research shows that intake of citrus fruits and juices helps lower anxiety.

Eat Foods that Boost the Production of serotonin: Serotonin is a neurotransmitter that triggers the mood enhancing portions of your brain thus reducing stress. The better the production of this hormone is in your body, the better you will fight anxiety. An easy way to accomplish this goal is to eat the various foods groups that boost its production. These foods include peanuts, chicken, soy products, seafood, and nuts. Incorporate these items into your diet to fight stage fright.

Exercise regularly: Exercise reduces cortisol levels in your body. Cortisol is a stress inducing neurotransmitter and works opposite to serotonin. By exercising regularly, you increase the production of serotonin and lower that of cortisol. With these changes occurring in your body, your mood starts elevating, which makes it easier to control your fears.

Sleep well: Research shows that if you sleep less than five hours every night, chances of suffering from anxiety increase. If you sleep less, this might be the reason behind your ever-increasing performance anxiety. To curb anxiety, it is important to get a good night's rest, daily. If you have started eating healthy and exercising regularly, your sleep will naturally become regulated and you'll be able to manage insomnia.

With time, these lifestyle changes will marginally reduce your stage fright.

View your anxiety as excitement

Another helpful technique that can help you deal with stage fright is to start viewing anxiety as an excitement. A study carried out by the Harvard Business School discovered that anxiety is a very strange emotion. The moment you start viewing your anxiousness as your excitement, it stops scaring you.

Whenever you are in a social or public situation that elicits the fear of public speaking, start telling yourself that it is not nervousness; rather, it is excitement building inside you. This simple realization will quickly mitigate your anxiety and make you speak easily.

Tell yourself that people are not here to listen to you

Often, we become scared of facing a crowd and speaking in front of it because we fear being judged. Well, you can tell yourself that they aren't gathered to listen to you, and are only here to hear a speech on a certain topic. Once you comfort yourself by saying this, you will start becoming relaxed because your mind will understand that it is not you the people want to see. You simply have a duty to perform and that's it. This will help you manage your phobia and speak successfully.

Focus on your audience and your material

A good tactic to overcome chronic stage fright is to shift your focus from your inner self to your audience and your material. We often become frightened of speaking publicly because of self-doubt. The reality is that your audience doesn't really care about your problems.

It is interested in what you present and how you present it. If you bear this point in mind, your anxiety will start decreasing. Focus on creating compelling content suited to your audience needs, so that your audience becomes attentive, and listen.

Implement these performance anxiety tips to boost your self-esteem and gather the confidence to speak in a conference and in front of all types of crowds.

Chapter 7: Asking Him or Her for a Date

Summary

It is considered to be a very difficult thing to do. Asking someone for a date. Probably because there are just two definite answers here – "yes' and "no'.

Asking Him or Her for a Date

Let me make clear here, right from the start. In this chapter, and in all the chapters that follow, what I am going to tell you is how to start talking with people. Or, rather, how to get people talking with you. However, no one can guarantee the results of such communication. There are many factors at play when you talk. No one can tell you what will happen as a consequence. But at the same time you have to know that most fruitful opportunities are lost just because people don't start the communication. So, when you learn how to talk with people, how to break the ice, you are already improving your playing field.

People think approaching someone for a date is a very difficult task. However, if you go about it the right way, you will at least be able to open the conversation and know if it is a "yes' or "no'.

Here are the steps you can use to go about it.

1. Be confident. Think how you will open up the conversation. If the boy or girl you are approaching has some common link with you, you could have something to talk about in that context. Otherwise, you could speak about the situation in which you find each other. Like, if you see him or her sitting at the food plaza in a mall and eating alone, you could walk up to him or her and ask, "Hello, could I join you? I have seen you eating alone here often." Yes, being honest works here. If you have seen them, you have seen them.

2. Always keep taking the hints. If they like you, it will be an immediate "yes'. A

reluctant "yes' will mean that you have to work on it. A "no' means you have to move elsewhere.

3. If you are sitting with them, keep foraging for topics to talk about. Don't worry; the communication lines are open now. You now have to observe the hints. If they like something, talk about it. Don't downgrade it right away. That could mean a polite excuse and the end of the conversation.

4. Plan in advance where you will ask them if the situation for a date seems to form itself. Ask them casually. Ask them, "Have you been to China Joe? I hear that's a good Chinese place to eat." If they say they haven't, ask them if they are interested in Chinese food. Basically, get to know them. Chances are, if they like you they will say "yes' to accompany you even if they don't like Chinese.

5. Start small. Don't plan an elaborate date right from the start. They will be more at peace to accompany you at a fast

food outlet first than at a seven course buffet restaurant. Also, for the first date choose a place where you can get some privacy but not too much privacy. That might scare them.

Most importantly, stay confident. It isn't going to be the end of the world if they say "no'. If at any point in the conversation they refuse, don't be depressed. It is their loss, not yours! Tell yourself that and move on!

CHAPTER 8: PURPOSE, IMPORTANCE, AND PRINCIPLES OF COMMUNICATION

Have you ever wondered what the importance of communication today is? For many people, communication has a similar relevance to breathing or eating. In general, its importance not only derives from its daily usefulness to talk with our relatives or friends, but it is so important that it plays a fundamental role in the survival of our species.

Defined as the process of sending and receiving information between two or more people, human communication comprises different types of interrelation, either personally or through digital channels. Although we will not address a detailed account of the importance of each of the channels and forms of communication, we will deepen aspects such as their impact on personal life and organizations.

Influence what we think of ourselves and others.

We all share the need to interact with other human beings. Communication can be understood as the process of understanding and sharing some idea. We transmit a message not only through what we say, but how we say it, either verbally or in writing. What do you think your life would be like if you couldn't communicate, if you couldn't ask for what you need, or understand the needs of others?

Being unable to communicate can even mean in many ways, losing a part of yourself; your ability to communicate is central to your self-concept. Everything communicates, our writing, the brands we wear, the language we use, the state of our clothes, the jewellery we use, the tattoos we have, our posture and gestures, everything! And at the same time, all this constitutes the concept we have of ourselves.

On the other hand, your communication skills are a great tool to understand others. Again, not only their words but their nonverbal language can provide you with very clear clues as to who they are and what their values and interests are. Active listening is also a good communicator's ability.

Communcation helps us teach and learn.

Another advantage of communication is that it helps us spread knowledge and information among people. For example, writers publish a book to share their experience with readers, teachers transmit their teachings with students, friends, and colleagues discuss their ideas with each other and companies interact with consumers. In addition, the Internet boom not only allows us to have access to information of all kinds but also makes it easier to have closer contact with people around the world. Without a doubt, the process of sharing knowledge and information would not be possible without communication.

The pillar of any relationship.

Human relationships are achieved through communication. This process helps people express their ideas and allows them to understand their emotions through others. As a result, we can develop feelings of affection or hate towards others and create positive or negative relationships.

The essential tool for all living beings.

The communication process is also a vital aspect of animals. All agencies need communication to cover their most basic needs, such as feeding, reproducing or protecting themselves from predators.

To conclude we can say that every day we are immersed in the communication process, whether we realize it or not. Every aspect of nature, be it animals, plants, humans and even the weather, transmits messages that can be understood and interpreted through observation. Being in touch with our surroundings and receptive to what is transmitted to us is crucial for us to evolve day by day.

Importance of Communication in personal life

To talk about the importance of communication for life implies referring to its relevance in the role, work, profession, or trade that each one exercises as part of his or her life.

For example, many researchers write articles to make the world known about their latest discoveries and theories. Without proper communication, scientific development would be impossible. On the other hand, in the case of families that live far away, the latest advances in communication allow parents and children, siblings or couples to keep in touch without having to face each other or in the same place.

Moreover, the importance of communication in the social field is based on the fact that it is the basis of every human relationship. In the beginning, we are all strangers to each other, but as we interact and interact with other people we begin to form interpersonal bonds that are formed thanks to communicative actions.

In this sense, in such an interconnected world, it is necessary that we begin to acquire good practices of effective and assertive communication.

Importance of Communication in organizations

At the business level, communication processes are of vital importance for the development of organizations. One of the main reasons is explained by the fact that communication is the backbone of every company. But what exactly does this mean?

Every organization requires a constant flow of information in order to perform its most basic functions. For example, in a medium-sized restaurant, it is necessary that waiters and cooks are constantly being informed about the dishes that customers ask for. If an order is badly given or if the information does not arrive from the waiter to the cook, it is most likely that serious problems arise with customers that could have negative consequences for the company.

Without a good flow of information, it is inevitable that conflicts arise between areas, employees, and bosses, and even between co-workers.

At present, there are specialties such as Internal Communication and Labor Communication that are specifically responsible for promoting good communication between our employees, employees and internal clients. This is an additional aspect that shows us the importance of communication in organizations.

Examples of the Importance of Communication

A classic example that allows us to reflect on this issue is when two people who speak different languages try to start a conversation. In this case, communication can play an essential role if a person has an urgent problem that he cannot solve alone and needs help, or also when two or more people want to talk about business, but do not have a common language.

Another important example will be seen when two people are from different cultures and have conflicts. In these cases, communication is absolutely necessary to develop reconciliation and problem-solving processes. Here we refer specifically to Intercultural Communication, which is a sub-frame of Human Communication focused on communicative processes in dissonant cultural environments.

A third example that allows us to understand better the importance of communication is when we try to sell a product or service. As we know, every advertising campaign requires a solid communication base: who are we addressing, how, when, where, among others. If we do not take into account the communicational aspects of what we want to offer, most likely, our business idea will fail.

Also, at the labor level, communication is essential to be able to perform our duties as employees or bosses properly. Without assertive communication, it is very certain that our projects fail, that we have constant discussions in our work area and that we can even be fired or that our company loses profitability.

Another case that demonstrates how important communication is is when the government does not carry out communication actions that inform people about the work they are doing. Without good government communication, citizens may lose confidence in rulers, as well as in-state institutions, which can lead to political complications.

Finally, the communication of our ideas and feelings is necessary to maintain emotiona stability. At the intrapersonal level, communication has a priority role in keeping us healthy and leading a calm and quality life.

Chapter 9: Networking Effectively Through Communication

What is networking? Networking is interacting with other people in order to exchange information or develop contacts, particularly to help further your career. How can effective communication help you network? We've got you covered.

Be Professional

First and foremost, networking is about selling yourself. In order to do that, you need to make sure you come across as desirable as possible. This means not only always dressing the part, but making sure the things you say carry weight in a business-like manner. Whether in person or on the phone, make sure the words that escape your mouth are proper with no slang or expletives. Be sure to use phrases that show your intelligence, but be certain that the words you use are the correct ones for the message you are trying to get across. If you are unsure, use an alternative word. Your body language comes into play here as well. If you slouch and mumble at the floor you will certainly make an impression, but not the right one. Remember to stand tall and speak with authority. Your confidence and surety are sure to be remembered and there is a chance your name will be passed along to others, widening your net.

Plan

In life, we are always told that we should have goals. The same goes for effectively communicating to people. You should, when going into a meeting, always have a goal set. Have an idea of what you want to accomplish. It does not hurt to write down what you want to say, or, at least, a basic outline of what you are trying to get across. Try to focus on what you have to offer to the people listening to you, not what you can get from them. What you have to give is going to stand out more to them than what you are asking for. Know your audience. If you want to get something from someone, you want to research the best way to go about it. Play to your strengths and play to your audience, always. Do not be afraid to be bold within reason.

You are the Product

Networking is essentially selling you to others. What is it that makes you stand out, what about your personality is going to stick in their minds? This is why the way you speak and hold yourself is so important. Again, body language plays a large part in your success. Listen inventively to the speaker, and answer all questions as fully as possible. Put yourself or your product out there plainly, make it crystal clear what it is you are trying to accomplish with this networking. Shake hands with them. Try to stand out in good ways, not because your clothes are dirty or you smell like you haven't showered in days. Effective communication also is about confidence. Be confident, stand up straight, and sell yourself before you even open your mouth. Sometimes what you didn't say is more important than what you did.

Play Fair

While it is true you want to stand out and show off your talents, you do not want to do this by putting others down. Do not be that person. If you cannot showcase yourself without knocking someone else down, then you need to start over and take another look at the way you treat people. Remember that communication is not just about speaking, but respect as well. In some cases, it would be a good idea to actually talk up your competition. This will make it look as though you relish the challenge but you are not intimidated by your opponent. It will also offer the people you are trying to impress the idea that you respect your competition. Do not be the guy who slings mud, leave that to someone else. Be honest, respectful, and courteous and you are sure to catch the attention of those you are looking to impress.

Occasionally, you can use your words to change minds and steer situations in the direction you want them to go. This is called persuasion and it is a very powerful tool. While it is used predominantly in marketing and sales, there are a few of the principles you can apply to your home life as well.

Chapter 10: Prepare to Fight

Preparation is the best ammunition against fear. Getting prepared for a battle is preparing to win. To overcome your fear of public speaking, you have to learn your way around and through it to thwart the very fear of being embarrassed or getting caught off guard in public.

Preparation has two parts: preparing the speech and preparing to speak. Each of them does not work without the other. Mastering both will make you an expert to be lauded by the public instead of being ridiculed.

Learn to prepare everything there is to prepare.

Understand your topic

You have to master it like your whole career, livelihood and future depend on it. Take a great salesman, who is technically an expert when it comes to conversing and persuading, as an example. A salesman undergoes months of training to totally understand a product down to the last details. When combined with a charming personality, he is sure to excel in his chosen field and rake a lot of money.

Knowing as much as possible about your topic lessens your chances of committing a mistake and getting lost. It also makes bouncing back faster.

Organize all your materials

Your presentation routine needs to be well-choreographed to work. What materials will you use? Do you need visual aids, power point presentations, audios, props or assistants? Place them all on schedule according to the construction of your presentation. Knowing the exact timing when they are needed gives you a clear picture of what to take place from start to finish. It beats the very fear of not knowing what to happen, so it will relieve you a lot.

Plan transitions

Jumping from one topic to another or one section to another without smooth transition is awkward. Remember, awkwardness marks the onset of embarrassment. To avoid getting into an awkward situation, plan your transitions very well.

You can use a funny anecdote to lighten up the mood after a 10 minute spiel using formal tone. If you are transitioning from one visual aid to another, you can move out of the podium and move toward the middle of the stage to prevent a down moment. If you feel like an assistant arranging props on stage while you are delivering is awkward, why not crack a joke out of it?

Preparing a joke or rehearsing a funny line can also be your life support should you get lost or go blank for a moment. When you are into public speaking, remind yourself that you are like a radio jockey – you can pause, but you can't have dead air.

Likewise, you should also prepare an "escape line" should you be caught off guard by an audience who asks a question you don't know the answer to. Say something like "You know what, let's ask other audiences to know what they think about that" and from their answers, you can form your own opinion. Or, confirm that you are not sure about the answer and start your answer instead with an "I think..." That way, they'll know it is some sort of a disclaimer.

Learn body language

Do a research. Like a theater actor, you should know how to act and react on stage. You need to know what actions are appropriate, over-the-top and offending. Talking in front of people like a static recording machine is a big boo-boo.

Body language also refers to movements. Plan your blocking. Which side of the stage should you be facing on this part? Should you start discussing behind the podium or on the middle of the stage? Are you planning to stay behind the podium all the time (recommended only for formal speeches)?

Just a tip: when you are discussing a strong point or the highlights of your speech, move towards the front of the stage, closer to the audience.

Prepare to see disconnection and inattention

For sure, at least once in your life, you've been to an event you attended because you were forced to. It happens in school – principal's requirement; in corporate event – boss' requirement; in family reunion – mother's requirement; and in church – the congregation expects you to.

Don't expect that all your audience is there to listen to you wholeheartedly. Some of them are just invited by close friends they couldn't say no to. Some are there for the snacks. Some are there to observe. What matters is not what they feel before you start talking. What matters is what they feel while and after you are talking.

CHAPTER 11: Structure of This Work:

Clearing the Past, Present and Future

Clearing the path towards possessing a positive self-image as a speaker-performer will involve work on several levels. Something triggered this into being an issue for you, and by labeling it as a problem, you've been been inadvertently strengthening its power – even affirming it as a **truth** – ever since. While it's true that the past is over and done with, old painful memories may still be driving some of your subconscious programming even if you never consciously think about them. They can narrow the field of opportunities you notice, what you say 'yes' and 'no' to, and shape to what extent you allow yourself to dream and plan for the future.

In the next chapter, I will ask you to pick out some past experiences that stood out in your mind as you wrote the story of your issue. The fact that you remember much about them at all suggests that they're an important part of your identity as a public speaker-performer. Once the negative impact of those events has been cleared, you'll be more open to being in the spotlight.

We will move from the past to the present, where we examine your general mood about speaking? What do you need to be or do or have to become successful at this? Shedding light on the specific situations or audiences that you anticipate being a challenge will also be very useful in achieving the self-expression freedom you seek.

Having cleared the pull of the past and doubts about your abilities, in the final chapters we will work to strengthen your self image and pre-pave future presentations for success.

Chapter 12: Engaging Your Audience

Have you ever been in the crowd and listened to a speaker who just automatons on and on...? On the off chance that you have gone to school or worked in the corporate world, odds are you have. This is on account of in these situations; individuals are talked in light of their training, background, and position, not their capacity to talk. While it is incredible to have educated individuals speaking, the heartbreaking reaction is a group of people that is quite focusing, doesn't get the point, and may even nod off!

Talking is a work of art, and the capacity to keep a crowd of people drew in is basic to the speaker. One method of doing that is to utilize your voice as an instrument to attract the gathering of individuals. The word reference characterizes ramble as "to talk in a dull tone." Dull is marked as "told in an unvarying tone." Hence, on the off chance that you would prefer not to ramble on as a speaker, you should figure out how to change your tone.

Fluctuating your tone sounds sufficiently straightforward; simply stir up the volume, pitch, and speed of your discourse. The test is that while varying your tone sounds simple; it can be difficult to do. This happens for two reasons:

In our particular heads, when we talk, we have a tendency to hear how we think we sound. You may believe that you are shifting your voice a mess, however to a crowd of people you might be utterly dull.

You can wind up so centered around your substance and the words that you need to say that you may totally overlook or disregard the conveyance. This could be because of nerves, the absence of arrangement, unreliability, or numerous different things. In any case, once you disregard conveyance, you fall back on to whatever talking style you have dependably had. On the off chance that that happens to be a bit "ramble y," then you will exhaust your gathering of people.

The ultimate test is sufficiently simple to alter: Either record yourself talking and hear it out later (I know this can be agonizing. However it's precious!) or request original group of onlookers input from individuals you trust to give you legit yet valuable feedback. Joining a Toastmasters club is an incredible approach.

The second test is a considerable measure harder. How would you move some of your centers to conveyance when it's whatever you can do to control your apprehension and recall what you need to say next?

The primary path is to isolate content totally from the conveyance. To do this, utilization an improv drama method called "jabber." The drive is characterized as "confused or counter-intuitive talk."

permanently, put on a show to convey an address, yet rather than communicating in English (or whatever your local tongue is), speak in babble. Make a progression of illogical sounds as you put on a show to address a crowd of people.

Now, your substance is superfluous. As you do this address, indeed play around with the velocity, volume, and pitch of your voice. While doing this, honestly go "over the top" with it. Keep in mind, in your head you presumably think your assortment is much greater than it is. By utilizing jabber, you can center 100% on your conveyance.

When you get a tiny bit agreeable only playing with the assortment in nonsense, you can take it up an indent with a fun accomplice exercise called the Rubbish Master:

You will be a specialist on some basic, ordinary point. You will then convey an address on this theme, yet you will talk just in babble. After each couple of sentences, respite, and let your accomplice "interpret" what you just said in babble. In execution, there are comedic contrivances to make this activity more entertaining (i.e. you talk in nonsense for 45 seconds, and your accomplice interprets with a solitary word like, "consequently"). With the end goal of learning vocal assortment, you would prefer not. The objective here is to get your accomplice to decipher as accurately as could reasonably be expected what you are stating, utilizing only your tone and voice. You will tend to use your hands and body; This is fine to some extent, however, don't transform this into a round of pretenses. You ought to convey your rubbish as though the group of onlookers comprehended you. By honing this, you will pick up a comprehension of how to utilize the tone of your voice to pass on as much data as the words you say.

Chapter 13: Speech Body

If the speech introduction is the appetiser, then the body of the speech is the main course. This is where you present the meat of your message. Here is where you explain all, along with facts and reasons supporting your speech.

In essence, the speech body is where we "Tell them."

Here is where you present the points you want to make and where you provide your proof, data, or whatever will convince your audience. The body of the speech is the meat of your speech.

This chapter will teach you how to avoid a common mistake beginners make when giving a speech that makes their speech sound awkward and stilted.

You will learn a simple and quick method for writing the body of your speech.

Writing the Body of the Speech

Do not write out the whole speech word for word. Beginning speakers make this mistake. They will write out pages, paragraph after paragraph and try to memorize these pages word for word. This creates some challenges.

It is a lot to remember and chances are the speech giver will forget important points. This is usually causes awkward pauses and stumbling through the speech.

We write differently than we speak; a fully written speech will sound unnatural and stilted.

Fortunately, there is a much simpler way to write a speech so it sounds natural and makes it easier to remember the main points and supporting information. Write the speech body in point form.

Write the speech body in point form. On one line, write a phrase saying what you want your audience to remember. Below that, indented slightly, write a phrase that supports that point such as supporting material, a quote, reasons, etc.

~Main Point 1

--sub-point for main point 1; answer why

--supporting information for main point 1

~Main Point 2

--sub-point for main point 2; answer why

--supporting information for main point 2

~Main Point 3

--sub-point for main point 3; answer why

--supporting information for main point 3

Have no more than two or three main points for every 5-7 minutes of your speech. Less is more. It is far better to make the speech too short than too long.

Most audiences cannot absorb more information than two or three items.

Some people will tell you that you can present up to 5 points in a five-minute speech. I have always found presenting more than three points makes the speech feel rushed. An exception would be if you were simply listing a series of items with no explanation, like a series of household tips.

State one thing you want the audience to remember, followed by any data, reports, points, or arguments that support that point. Then do the same thing for two more points you want your audience to remember.

Good supporting materials are verifiable facts, diagrams, charts, statistics, stories or anecdotes and the opinions of experts in the field.

I found that five minutes of speech is roughly about one page of double spaced typing. I prefer to type my speech in Word using a large font and double spacing between lines. I indent for sub-points using the Tab key. The large font allows me to read my speech from an appropriate distance, and the double spacing leaves room for me to add corrections when needed.

Note that you do not have to follow the format given strictly. Use what works for you.

Obviously a speech can be handwritten. One problem I have with handwritten speeches is that my handwriting is terrible. I usually cannot read it afterwards!

Points Jog your Memory so You Remember Everything

One huge advantage of the point form method is that you already know the details of what you are going to say; you just need to remember to say it. You know all the details; a simple two or three word reminder is all you need to put down in the body of your speech.

The following is an example of how the entire details of two stories can be put into one or two simple points. Notice how long these stories are and how few words are needed to remember to tell them.

When I first began public speaking, it was at my church. I was terrified of making a mistake. Hence, I made no end of mistakes.

My second public speech ever was done in front of about 200 members of our congregation. While talking, I moved my right arm out to make a gesture. My arm went out to the right and then up ninety degrees due to my elbow being at a right angle. It would not go down or move no matter how much I willed it. That is how nervous I was. I gave the majority of my five minute speech like that. It looked ridiculous. Worse, my notes were in my right hand and now I could not read them! The notes made me look even sillier as the papers drooped over my right hand. The right hand attached to an immovable arm at a ninety degree angle.

Fortunately, I had rehearsed that speech many, many times. Unknown to me until that moment, I did not need the notes. I gave the rest of the speech from memory.

A speech or two later, I was sitting in church waiting for my turn to give a speech to about thirty people. My legs were crossed an unknown to me had fallen asleep. I walked to the podium and began to give my speech. My leg gave out and I landed over the podium, my body folded in two.

I picked myself up and noticed no one said a word, so I just continued on. My leg gave out again for the second time in five minutes. Again, I was completely draped over the podium!

I have to commend the congregation for what they did. They did precisely nothing. No reaction, no comments or teasing afterwards. They simply forgave it.

I had embarrassed myself beyond measure. And the audience did not care. I figured if an audience could forgive that, they would forgive almost anything. That realization drove away 90% of my stage fright.

People comment on how comfortable I am on stage. And generally I feel right at home on a stage speaking to the public. I love it. My comfort level is directly because of a blessing in disguise. A horribly embarrassing moment cured my stage fright.

See how long those two stories are? Telling them in person is quicker because I can demonstrate what my arm and body did; a picture truly is worth a thousand words.

Since I know each story in detail, I can remember both stories with simply a few words to nudge my memory. The arm-freezing story can be remembered by the words "arm freezing story". When I read "arm freezing story" my mind fills in all the details.

Similarly, the words "fell over podium story" brings back all the details of the time I fell over the podium twice in five minutes.

Example - How Problems can be Blessings

Here is how I wrote those two detailed stories in my speech notes on how problems can be blessings. The completely written speech is in the Appendix.

~arm freezing story

~fell over podium twice story

~I still try my best to give a good speech

--worry much less

--relax, enjoy giving speeches

When you know your material well, very few notes are needed to give a speech.

Example - Hotel Giving Outstanding Customer Service

Another example is a hotel that provides sterling customer service and wishes to remain a leader in the hospitality business. The completely written speech is in the Appendix.

~Question is "What can we do better?"

--prompts customers to tell what they did not like or what they thought could be done better

~Customers are a source of new ideas

--even if they were generally satisfied and liked our service

--often there is one thing people wish was different or better

--Customers know about our competitors' practices

--Customers have a variety of experiences; have seen the way different businesses are ran

~This allows us to continuously improve and stay as the hotel of choice for our clients.

--We will not know unless we ask.

Example - Engineer Recommending a Policy Change

A third example is an engineer recommending a change to a company's design policies. The completely written speech is in the Appendix.

~Recommend running components at <= 80% of maximum specification

--currently we are close to 100% of maximum specification

--Electronic parts run cooler, are less stressed

~they don't fail as often

--on pilot project, product returns decreased by 52% compared to similar product lines

--greatly reduces repair costs; repairs costs are only 20% of comparable product lines

~Customers are happier

--product is reliable

--they do not have to send it back for repair

--pilot product surveys show customer satisfaction increased by 83% compared to similar products

As you can see, this point form approach has advantages. It is very quick and easy.

Simply write down a point to present. Below it, indented slightly, write why it is important. Then write down a reminder about supporting information.

With practice, you can create a speech in a few minutes if need be.

It is also easier to memorize a few points than to remember several paragraphs word for word.

You are free to speak with your normal manner of speaking which gives authenticity to your speech. It makes your speech more real and natural to the audience.

Write these points as short phrases; detail is not necessary. Their purpose is to remind you of what you want to say. You will fill in the words when you give the speech. Simply write enough so you will know what you want to say.

How do you figure out what words to say when you give the body of your speech? Rehearsing takes care of this. Simply rehearse the speech several times. You will find the sentences you need when you begin to speak about the next point of your speech. It is just like when we speak naturally in conversation. We know what we want to say, and the words come out of our mouths naturally. The wording may very slightly each time we say it, but the message stays the same. Read the chapter on rehearsing the speech for more about this.

Long Speeches

What is the speech is longer than 5 minutes? What do you do if your speech is fifteen minutes long?

Simply use the above method and provide either more supporting evidence or more points of value to the audience. Using the 2-3 points/5-minutes guideline, a fifteen minute speech will have about 6-9 points presented. Alternatively, present the supporting information more in-depth. It depends on your speech and on what you want the audience to take away with them.

What do you do if your speech is four hours long? If you are speaking for four hours, the chances are you need to be a more advanced speaker than is covered in the scope of this book. However, I did successfully give several four-hour speeches when I was a beginning speaker by adapting the methods shown in this book.

I once taught evening college courses in electronics. At the time, I have never given more than a five-minute speech in my life. I created a very simple method of presenting information to the class.

I wrote various pieces of my lesson (speech) in five-minute increments. Each increment had two or three talking points. Each took up about a page of double spaced typing. There were many pages!

There is no way to remember four hours of speaking, so I put the notes in a binder and used it as my guide. I would glance at the page and give a speech on that page. Then I would turn to the next page and give a speech on that page. It was a very effective way to teach. Of course, it helps that I was an expert in electronics. I knew my subject.

At each 5-minute interval, I put the length of time it should have taken to reach that part of the speech (1:35 for one hour and thirty-five minutes). Adding the length of time to the start time (classes started at 6:00 PM) let me know if I was on track. 6:00PM plus my 1:35 marker told me I should be that spot in the lesson at 7:35 PM.

Alternatively, I could have written the actual time 7:35PM instead to avoid the math. However, since I wanted to teach the course again and again, I did not use this approach.

If I was behind schedule, I simply skipped sub-points or more in-depth discussion until I was back on track.

Professional training companies use a similar method. They have a binder filled with notes that the trainers use. They position a clock where the speaker can easily see it but the audience cannot. This keeps the Trainer on time.

Summary

The speech body is where we "Tell them." It is the meat of your speech.

Present the points you want to make and provide your supporting information. Use short phrases that merely remind you of what you want to say.

One double spaced typewritten page will make a speech that is about 5 minutes long.

On a piece of paper or in a word processor, use the following format:

~Main Point 1

--sub-point for main point 1; answer why

--supporting information for main point 1

~Main Point 2

--sub-point for main point 2; answer why

--supporting information for main point 2

~Main Point 3

--sub-point for main point 3; answer why

--supporting information for main point 3

Have only two or three points for every 5 to 7 minutes of your speech. Less is more.

If you have a long speech to give, write it in several 5-minute speech segments.

Chapter 14: DO YOUR HOMEWORK. THEN DO THE EXTRA CREDIT.

The speech or presentation is not about you. If you think it is, you're in trouble. The faster you understand this, the better you will be as a public speaker. Your audience has not asked for much. They want you train them. They want you to be original. They want your presence. They want your success. You can deliver on these expectations. You do so by making the presentation all about them.

A vast majority of the work is done before your presentation begins. You can and should "Wow" your audience with your knowledge of who they are, why they are here, and what they want to learn. It is all about them. It is not about you. If you do not enjoy public speaking, this is more good news. Knowing your audience has more to do with preparation than public speaking skills. More preparing, less stress and anxiety. Less stress and anxiety, better public speaking performance. More preparation equals better public speaking performance.

I will illustrate with a real-life example. I recently gave a public speaking training to an array of corporate executives in San Francisco. 50 executives were expected to attend. Public speaking is a broad topic, so I wanted to know more about the audience. I emailed the event organizer a survey to send a dozen of the participants to complete ahead of time. This would help me understand their specific needs and goals for the event. Their feedback showed me the number one goal for the training was to use public speaking to inspire their managers to produce more results. I tailored the training to these objectives. Imagine if I had not reached out, and spent the majority of the training on the basics of public speaking like eye contact, posture, and vocal tone on stage. Would this content show I understood my audience? NO! I would have instantly frustrated them. The good-will they granted me would have disappeared. They wanted to learn about motivating their management teams. Posture and eye contact had little to do with that goal.

The post-presentation feedback I received was positive. A few attendees hired me to coach them privately. Each person that hired me told me they did so because my content focused on an understanding of their struggles and provided solutions. In other words, my preparation, not my public speaking skills, led to increased business. If I failed to do my homework, I would have missed this opportunity.

Many speakers panic and ask me, "What is the best way to know what your audience wants?" The answer is obvious, but almost never implemented. The best way to know what your audience wants is to ask them. In many cases, you have direct access to the people that come to your meeting or event. In situations where you have limited or no access to the audience, you can work with the event or conference organizer. It is their job to serve as the bridge between your audience and you. I suggest asking no more than three questions of your audience to clarify their needs. People are busy. If you send them more than three questions, it gets overwhelming. Keep it simple. For example, I created the following survey for the above-mentioned public speaking training I led in San Francisco. The organizer emailed the participants these questions a few weeks before the training:

What is your biggest frustration with public speaking?

Why do you want to improve your public speaking skills?

What have you tried in the past to become a better public speaker?

Each audience will require different questions, but the takeaway here is universal. Do not assume you know what your audience wants to learn. Do not assume you know their major struggles. Understand what they hope to learn.

Understand why they are frustrated. Understand what they have tried in the past. Then you can provide solutions. Your audience will appreciate this. Your mind will be at ease because you know you are teaching them exactly what they want to learn. You don't have to and shouldn't ever enter a presentation blind. There is no need to throw random objects, ideas, or solutions at the wall and hope something sticks. You should already know. Knowledge is power. Knowledge will set you free. Stop guessing. Stop assuming Public speaking is hard enough as it is.

In addition to the information you can gather in the days or weeks before the event, there is another step you can take to ensure you "Wow" your audience. If it's possible and appropriate, show up before the speech and talk to the participants. If you are speaking at a conference, hang out at the bar the night before. Plan a group dinner with the organizers and some VIP participants at a local restaurant.

Arrive at your presentation 30 minutes early and chat with the attendees. This allows you to meet your audiences and ask them questions. These conversations provide you with training material. You also build your relationship and goodwill with your future audience. People want to follow leaders who are approachable, trustworthy, and human. People do business with those they like, respect, and trust. A little effort, preparation, and face time will show your audience you are all of those things. Set yourself up to succeed before you even step foot on the stage. Preparation is an excellent speaker's best friend.

CHAPTER 15: Speak About What You Know

One of the best tactics when it comes to engaging in public speaking is to first discuss things that you are thoroughly familiar with.

For example, Joe was then assigned to write and then present a persuasive speech; because Joe was passionate about football, and believes that most women would appreciate the game too, he has decided he will write a persuasive speech and focus his content on things that can influence women to consider watching football as well.

This could actually be a difficult speech to write, but if you have expertise, it will be significantly easier to convince your audience because of your knowledge base.

The only other exception to writing speeches and presenting them if you do not understand the content would be for you to do research on till you do.

Sharing things that you're genuinely passionate about, can actually be quite contagious for the people listening to your speech. This is particularly useful if you have a special kind of insight or even an event that has happened in your life that gives credence to the speech that you are presenting.

Once you have thoroughly researched and are presenting contents that you completely understand, the next steps are working on cadence, presentation and delivery.

Start Practicing In Front Of the Mirror & Timing

Now that you've done your research, understand exactly what you want to say, it's time to work on how to say it and that can only be done with practice, practice, practice!

After writing your speech, the first thing you need to do is read the speech out loud much the way that you would speak before other people. You should also time your speech because it is important to know exactly how long you should be talking and to rehearse until we were within 1 minute of delivering correctly the content that you want people to hear, and within the allotted time.

You should then give your speech again, and again watching your body language in the mirror. When you feel comfortable enough that you are willing to present your speech to others, offer to do so in front of family and friends. They can give you additional advice, tips and strategies based on what they see.

If you know of any good public speakers in your own network, invite them to any practice presentations and they can critique it for you.

Make sure you ask only for corrective feedback and continue to practice until your speech becomes more natural, comfortable for you to give and the majority of people who are giving you advice say that it sounds great.

Now Record Your Presentation

If you ever had the opportunity to take public speaking in school, college or business seminar, one of the best tools utilized is simply to video record your presentations. Not only is this interesting to see as your public skills continue to increase, but you can also share this video with friends and family and eventually other professional public speakers can then offer an honest evaluation of your growing public speaking skills.

Make sure that you take the time to record your entire body and that you can clearly hear the pitch and tone of your voice. This will let you see if you can clearly deliver and improve on the issues that are uncovered when you begin to record your speaking skills.

Don't worry! Many of us that started out in the public speaking arena were not very good at first. By taking the time to record your voice and body language, you can identify things like:

Annoying vocal tics (i.e. saying um, er, stuttering etc.)

Improper body language

The sound and cadence of your voice

Positioning of body parts when speaking

These are just some of the things that you will cover!

CHAPTER 16: EFFECTIVE INTRODUCTION

Introduction is the first thing you say to jumpstart your speech. It is like an actor entering the stage. His manner of entry has the potential to make or mar his performance for the day. Enter sluggishly and the audience will promptly conclude that you've nothing to offer. But, climb the podium brimming with zeal and enthusiasm, then see how everyone responds with eager expectation of what's to follow.

Again, damn good introduction is like opening the window to let your audience take a quick look at the items on display in the room. It should whet their appetite by doing a predetermined work. Yes, an effective speaker must take time to determine the exact work the introduction should do.

As a rule, a good introduction should arouse people's interest in the talk, clearly identify what you intend to talk about and show how the topic can help the listeners to fix one or two things that they consider important. Truth is, if the listener does not have an interest in the topic, or see clearly how it can affect his life, he isn't going to spend precious time listening to you, except he is compelled to listen by circumstances beyond control. For instance, employees are frequently made to spend precious long times hearing out a presentation by the chief executive officer of the company, even when he did not bother to show why the talk is important to the staff.

Points to note

Create an interest.

There are various ways to arouse interest of your listeners. We will proceed to discuss four ways frequently used by the masters of the art. One sure way to arouse interest in your speech is to ask a question or a series of question arising from the topic. These are questions that you intend to answer in the course of the speech. Others could be rhetorical designed to make people think about the subject. If you are discussing the high rate of divorce in America, for instance, you may ask: "Do you know how many couples that got divorced in the last one week in the United States? The number will amaze you!"

Many in the audience may be aware, or worried, about growing cases of marriage failures in the country, but few would ever have bothered about the weekly rate. The prospect of hearing the figure would likely make them to listen attentively as the talk unfolds.

The use questions to engage the audience during a public presentation is so important that we deem it fit to devote a chapter to it. So, we'd return to it in a short while.

If you do not have appropriate question to use in flagging off your speech, no need to worry. You can use another effective opening, like the telling of a real life story that may be known to you alone, or even known to a number of other persons in the audience. Using the example of the growing rate of marriage breakdowns across the nation, you may tell a story highlighting the negative impact of this social problem. Do you know of any woman who now suffers depression despite receiving huge sums of alimony following a successful divorce? It is sure to get people's attention.

There's one more thing you could do to raise audience attention at the beginning of your talk. It is to refer to a current news item, related to your theme, which particularly touched the community. For example, on the issue of marriage breakdowns, a good speaker could call attention to a recent case of divorce, perhaps, one involving a celebrity, along with huge payment of alimony to the wife.

The point is, no matter what theme you handle, there's always something in the news of recent, which could be cited to arouse the interest of those listening, that is, if you have no question and no real life experience to share.

You'd notice that we did not recommend that you kick off a presentation with one funny joke. The reason is, not many people have the gift of making others laugh. Believe it or not, it's not always the story itself that elicits laughter. It is the style of narration that makes people laugh. Some persons are so humorous that mere sight of them throws up a smile on many faces.

If you do not belong to the class of notable comedians, it's advisable to strongly resist the urge to start a talk with a joke. It rarely turns out well for the masters of the art; and it is always a guaranteed disaster for rookies. Please, forget the joke, except if you were specifically hired to dish them. Define the topic.

A good introduction should be an executive summary of the talk. It should include the theme, a number of the sub themes and some of the supporting lines of thought, all combined in a manner that makes clear the significance of the subject.

Suspense is not a virtue in public speaking. It is acceptable in novels and creative writings. In those literary genres, suspense is employed to keep the highpoint of the story hidden to a reasonable extent, so the reader keeps wondering, or imagining how the key characters would wriggle out of the web of intricate plots and scenes.

This is not the case with public address. No. You don't keep the audience guessing about the subject, or purpose, of your talk. Even your spouse in the room would feel frustrated and opt out of it, if you deploy suspense in family discussion, as in dancing around the topic for unduly long time!

To retain an interest in your speech, you must quickly make the issues clear to everyone. They need to know the scope and purpose of your talk, which must be of real and immediate benefit to them. A good introduction to a public talk must, therefore, define the topic in clear terms.

As an introduction to a short talk on the need for married couples to appreciate kind deeds of their mates, the speaker said, "Ladies and gentlemen, in the next 15 minutes, we'd see why it's important to appreciate your mates. We'd examine three instances of people who did it and the fine results it brought. Then, we would review four practical ways in which you can show sincere appreciation."

Nothing is left to imagination. Everyone in the audience knows what is to be discussed, and for how long. Anyone with a notepad in hand can actually jot down the intro as their own outlines of the talk to help then follow as it unfolds.

Show why it matters.

The audience needs to know why your talk is important to them, or to anyone else. Will it help them live a healthier and happier life, gain more knowledge about a current event, or push their career to the next level? If you are ever going to succeed in getting the audience to agree with you that your subject is important, you must strive to adapt the talk to the practical needs of the people.

It is very normal for people to pay attention to materials that address their fears, challenges and aspirations. And how can you adapt your material to suit the audience, if you did not have fore knowledge of the sort of conditions that prevail among them? So, as part of your preparation for the presentation, you make effort to find out what's going on in the lives of the people that would be listening to you.

Mind your language

The way you start the talk sends early signals about you and your proficiency or ineptitude. Let us limit ourselves here to your choice of words. It pays to start with simple words, familiar phrases and uncomplicated sentences. If you chose to write down what you'd say for a start, go for short paragraphs as well, since paragraphs have a way of showing themselves in speech, through longer pauses.

As a rookie in the art, it's tempting to believe that the so-called big words, complicated sentence structures and unfamiliar terms are signs of good education, academic excellence and soundness of mind. Truth is, speaking above the heads of the audience would cause offence, dampen interest, becloud meaning and block the flow of message from you to the audience. To avoid disaster, especially at the opening stages of your talk, do all you can to use words that are clear, simple and easy to understand.

You may not believe it, but it's very true that your audience would rather love it when you buy things, than when you purchase them. Many would be glad if you kindly help them to start an assignment, do it well; instead of you commencing it and executing it satisfactorily.

Did you catch the drift? We hope you'd agree that doing things well sounds better to the ears and coveys more meaning than executing tasks satisfactorily. That means, when you speak, you should never use a big word in place of a smaller alternative.

Now, you are through with your introduction. You've generated a wave of interest in your presentation. People are all years; all eyes on you. You've defined the topic in clear terms and showed why it matters and why people should spend precious time to listen to it. And you've done all these, using simple words, clear and easy to understand. Hey, you are on your way to delivering a great speech!

CHAPTER 17: The three very best places where the best topics are easy to find

If you already have the topic, then that's fine. However, if you need one, now or in the future, you can never go past these three resources.

The good thing about these places, is that they are always current. You will also be able to pick topics that you know a lot of people will be interested in. There's no point in giving a public talk on something very few, or no-one is interested in. So let's get to it.

The person who must be interested

If someone was to give you a topic that you were not interested in, you would find it hard. Also, your disinterest would come across to your audience. Your talk would be a complete failure.

You need to first start with yourself. You need to pick a subject that you have a personal interest in. If possible, you should be passionate about it.

For example, I could talk for hours and hours about writing. It's what I've done for years and have a passion for. I read just about anything I can get my hands on about the subject. I also love talking to other writers.

Of course, I also have many other interests. However, although these other things are not my passion, I am still interested in them. It's true to say that most people have more than one interest.

Whatever topic you choose for your talk, make sure it's one that you are personally interested in. By having an interest in the subject, you find it easier to talk about it. Your audience will also see your interest.

The perfect topic library

When finding public speaking topics you could do nothing else but this one thing. You will never run out of ideas. You are also guaranteed to have a large audience will be interested in it. Where?

By doing this first, you will see what the most popular subjects are. This will assure you that most people are interested in them. Take a look through this list and take notice of any books you have a personal interest in.

At this moment, three of the top subjects are...

Diabetes

Healthy eating

Weight loss

On the home page, select books and then click on the best sellers link at the top. This will give you the top one hundred best selling books.

If the subject is too broad, for your public speaking event, then narrow it down.

Here is the best way of doing it. Go to each book, or books, you find and take a look at the table of contents. You will see chapters focusing on different aspects of the subject. This will give you an awful lot more topics to consider. However, I suggest you go one step further.

Don't limit your choice of subjects to one or two books. Use Amazon's list of categories to bring up more books on the same subject.

On the left-hand side of Amazon's book page, you will see a list of categories. Click on a category which is focused on this subject. When you do this more subcategories will show up. Once again, click on one or more of these to narrow down the focus to your subject. You will end up with a list of the top one hundred best selling books about the subject you've chosen. If necessary, click on the 'look inside' feature of each book to view the table of contents.

You will get lots of topic ideas from this method. If you like, you could buy one or two of these books as a basis of research. However, don't copy what you read. Instead, learn from them. You will quite often find new ideas and strategies that you can teach on to your audience. In your own words of course.

Here's is an example...

When I looked at just one book about diabetes, I got these subtopics...

Curing diabetes

Understanding diabetes

Diets for diabetics

Menus and recipes for diabetics

Fat and diabetes

Five topics for a talk just from one book's table of contents. Depending on the proposed length of your speaking event, you could cover several of these topics.

Now do you think that some diabetics will be interested in these topics? I can tell you that a lot of them will. How do I know that? Because, at the time of writing, this book is the third best selling book out of all non-fiction books on Amazon.

I then brought up more books about this diabetes. I found them in the Amazon category: Health, Fitness & Dieting – Aging – Diabetes. I had in front of me the list of the top one hundred best sellers about this subject. Lots of ideas to use right there.

When you look through the titles and contents pages of these books, it will give you more than enough topics for your talk. The bonus is that all these books are best sellers. This shows the topics are all in demand.

Incidentally, there were also two other categories in which books on this subject appeared in. I'll show you the short-cut I used to find them.

What I did was go to the book sales page. The same one you go to in order to look inside at the table of contents.

Just below the book description you will see a section entitled 'Product Details'. It will give you the best seller rank for the book in different categories on Amazon. It will have the heading 'Amazon Best Sellers Rank'. Each category link shows in which category the book appears in the top one hundred best sellers. Simply click on each link and it will display the top one hundred best sellers for that category.

The diabetes book showed up in three categories. However, a book will usually only show in two.

This is the top way of finding the best topics for your public speaking event. Make full use of it.

Spy on your audience

Now for a bit of espionage. Well not really. But you can go and listen in to what your audience are talking about.

Go to forums about the subject you have chosen. If you don't have one, then pick a forum around a broad subject. Things like health, hobbies, and money. Starting broad will allow you to see the major interest areas and then narrow them down.

In each forum, you can search for questions. You should also take a look to see which posts are getting the most views and/or comments. This will show which ones are of most interest to people.

You can nearly always sort by date order. This is a good idea as you want to look at the most recent comments as they will show what the current interest is in. Topics come and go out fashion all the time. You want to make sure you are up to date with the latest trends.

Take a look at each post and read through the comments. By doing this, you will learn a lot about what people are interested in.

You will discover the problems people have. Problems are great opportunities for topics or sub-topics for your talk. We all want solutions to our problems. The bigger the problem, the more they'll be interested in a solution. Problems are a goldmine.

Think about it. If someone lies in bed at night worrying about something, you can bet they will be very interested in any possible solutions. If your talk is offering a solution, then you are sure to have many people interested in your talk.

Look for questions. This is your audience asking for information. It's what they want to know. The more people asking for the same answers, the more who are likely to attend your public speaking event.

Search in the forum's search box for phrases like...

Please help

Does anyone know

I have a problem

How can I

How do you

Phrases often begin with words like these when someone has a question they want answered. Often it's a problem. This is what you are looking for.

Try searches for as many of these types of phrases. Think about what words someone is likely to start with when searching for answers.

On a diabetes forum, this is what I found when I searched for the phrase 'how do you'...

How do you stay healthy during the holiday?

How do you handle fructose?

How do you handle your diabetes at Christmas?

How do you know if you are insulin resistant?

How do you live with diabetes?

This was just on page one.

You could then search further for questions about the same thing. This will tell you how popular it is. The more popular, the more interest.

Stick to up to date and busy forums. There are forums that are like ghost ships. Hardly anyone goes to them. You can easily spot them. There will either have no recent comments or very few. Remember, you want to know what people are looking for now. Not last year.

The fastest way to find forums

There is a little search technique that I've found to work very well.

The common advice, is to do a Google search for your subject word and add the word 'forum'. What I've found is that this brings up a lot of websites that are not forums. Sites that have the word forum anywhere in them. This wastes a lot of time.

What you do, is almost the same, but you use a little Google search code as well. Here is what you search for...

(Subject word) inurl:forum

The code, 'inurl:', tells Google to bring up websites where the word forum appears in its address. This means nearly all the results will actually be forums. Try it. It works!

For example, if you were searching for forums around the subject of diabetes, your search would be...

diabetes inurl:forum

You will find that you avoid nearly all non-forum websites.

How to quickly find a lot of questions your audience has

When you give your talk, you will get a lot more interest if you are answering the questions most of your audience have. You will also make your talk easier to plan. You will just need to make a list of all the questions and then just answer them in your talk. Simple.

You can find some of these questions by visiting forums. However, when it comes to questions, I haven't found one place to beat one particular website. Which website?

It's, dah dah, Yahoo Answers.

If you've not heard of this website before, it's a huge database comprised of questions and answers. It's a very popular site where people post questions. Other members can then post answers to these questions.

Go to the Yahoo Answers website. Search for words related to your subject area.

I would strongly suggest you first narrow down your topic by doing the book search you learned about earlier. This will allow you to look at more specific questions. Questions you could answer in your talk.

Once again, you can sort the results into most recent first. This is important. You need to make sure you find what people want to know now.

Look for questions that keep coming up. The more often a question is asked, the more people wanting the answer.

Yahoo Answers has countless questions. I doubt you will have enough time to go through every question. There are new questions being added all the time.

Once again, I would recommend you always start with the book search first. This will narrow down your topic. Afterwards, go and look at the forums and Yahoo Answers to pinpoint what the specific issues and questions people have.

To summarise

By giving a public talk on these subjects and answering questions most people want answered, you are almost guaranteed to attract a large audience. Not just any audience. But one filled with people with a strong interest in your subject.

Always remember your primary goal That is, to help people make their lives better. Therefore, first find out what most people want to know.

CHAPTER 18: The far easier and better way to prepare your talk

The most common way to prepare a talk takes a long time and has problems as a result. One of which is difficulty remembering your words.

This is the better way.

When I was called upon to give my first ever talk, it was not a great experience. I had trouble remembering my words. The words I did remember, came over like a script. There was no sincerity. It sounded unnatural. Not only that, but it also took me a long time to prepare it.

The thing is, this talk was only five minutes long.

The biggest mistake people make, is trying to remember their talk word-for-word. Not only is this approach very difficult, but also foolhardy. Even if you remembered every word, your talk would end up sounding like a parrot. It would also sound insincere. Not good.

The other problem with this, is that it causes the bad type of fear. You forget your words, where you panic and your mind goes blank.

Here is a much better way. The result is that you don't need to remember your words. You will find that you can walk out on stage and simply talk to your audience. Just like you were talking to a friend. Sound good?

The better way is to rehearse your talk out loud, **but not word-for-word**. Your words will be different every time. Which is good. The only thing you need to remember is what points you are going to make and the solutions you are going to offer. Use whatever words come to mind. For example, you rehearse five times.

Each time, don't try to use the same words. Instead, you just explain it like you would to a friend in the same room. If you explained your points on five different occasions to different people each time, you wouldn't worry about using the same words. It's the same with this. Each time you rehearse out loud, imagine it's someone else. Just explain everything to them, but don't worry about the words. Just get your point across. The secret here is that you need to forget about what words to say.

The success, of your public speaking event, does not depend on the words you use. It depends on the message and information you give.

Here is what I suggest. After you have decided on the points, methods, systems, stories, answers, etc., practice talking out loud to an imaginary friend. Don't worry about what words you use. Just talk to your friend. Then do it again to another imagine friend and so on. Each time using whatever words you want. Forget about scripts. Get that idea out of your head.

I recommend you do this three to five times. This will be enough times to break you free of using set words. It will get you to remember the points instead. The message you want to give.

Don't just rehearse the entire talk from start to finish You should also do it for each point, method, procedure, story, etc. Rehearse each one out loud three to five times. Then when you've covered everything, rehearse your entire talk out loud.

Once again, the most important thing to remember, is to accept that words can be different each time. This way, when you go on stage, you won't be trying to remember a script. You will simply go out there and talk. Using whatever words you want. The words don't matter, the points do.

So to summarise. Explain each point out loud to an imaginary friend. Do this three to five times for each point. After you've gone through all your points, rehearse, out loud, your entire talk at least three to five times.

What you'll find is that you will sound a lot more sincere and natural. As a bonus, you will also be more relaxed because you won't need to worry about remembering a script.

Don't prepare and rehearse your talk the old way. Do it the easier way.

An easy way of getting all your points in the right order

This is one I used to struggle with. The hours I used to spend moving things around. There is a much easier way.

You put everything on a time-line. Everything is in a chain of events.

It makes sense. For example, you wouldn't tell people to put the cake mix in the oven before you've explained how to prepare the mixture.

Just think about when you would make use of each point you're going to teach. For example, in this book I am explaining all the skills and techniques you'd use to prepare your talk before talking about the room set up and giving the talk. Think about it. That's the order you would approach your talk. Prepare, set up the room, and give the talk. In that order.

What you can do, is think about the task and about what you would do first, then next, and so on. Then just put all your points and techniques next to each task.

Some subjects are more difficult to do this with. However, you can always fall back on the clock or calendar.

Take diabetes. If your talk was about nutrition for diabetics, you could start in the morning and run through the day. You may expand and decide to do this for each day of the week. You'd go from Monday to Sunday, running from morning to night for each day. Simply place the nutritional tips, diets, and methods to the time they will be needed.

If your talk was about fishing, your timeline would start when you start planning the trip. This is where you would put your information about finding places to go. If your talk was for beginners, your time-line would start earlier when they are deciding what type of fishing they want to do. Next up would be buying the equipment. And so on.

Use the time-line to organise your points. You'll find it a lot easier.

The right time length that gives the best results

Imagine someone gave you the instructions for how to build a website. They spoke very fast, didn't pause and didn't allow you time to ask any questions. How would you get on?

You are going to be giving useful information in your talk. Therefore, if you rush through your talk, your audience will not have time to digest what you say. You will also not have the important pauses you'll learn about later. You'll also be flustered, continually wondering if you're going to have enough time to cover everything.

Your talk will be a lot better received if you take your time. Plus, you will find it a lot easier. Do it the right way with the right length.

Plan your talk to last for a slightly shorter time than is available. This is a simple idea that will do wonders for your talk.

When you know you have longer than you need, you will be more relaxed. This will transfer across to your audience.

If your talk is going to be for two hours, prepare information that can be done in one hour and forty five minutes. Prepare for fifty minutes when you have an hour. This extra time allowance will relax you and give you time to give quality instead of quantity. Quality is remembered: quantity is forgotten.

So take my advice, prepare your talk to fit into a shorter time frame.

To summarise

Plan your speech by rehearsing everything out loud.

Forget about which words to use. Put your points in order using the time-line technique.

Finally, prepare your talk to fit into a shorter time frame.

Chapter 19: How to control the audience

interaction

Take care of your appearance

You should look neat, handsome and good looking during the presentation day.

If your presentation is more than 4 hours, take a middle break and look to yourself in the mirror and prepare again for the rest of the presentation.

Keep smiley face

Keep a smile on your face during the presentation except in the sad situations as described early.

This will leave a positive impression towards your presentation.

Watch your stand

You should stand while you are speaking and give your speech. Don't speak while you are sitting on a chair.

The stand should be the POWER STAND

during your speech

Open your chest, don't cross your legs or stick them together, don't shake or bend your body. Your backbone should be centered on your two legs.

Simple walk around is sometimes accepted.

Take care of your hands

You should **never** point to your higher level audience with your figure when you gesture during the presentation.

This is totally unacceptable action towards your superiors and it will definitely leave a negative impression.

Also don't cross your hands during the presentation.

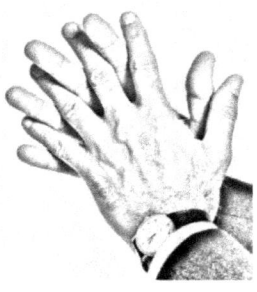

It will give negative impression that you are uncomfortable or have an inner fear.

Don't put your hands in your pocket

Putting your hand in your pocket is often considered arrogance.

It will definitely give a negative impression to the audience as if you are arrogant.

Putting your hand in your pocket while you are speaking will make the audience feel that you are in a higher level (of course it is negative action). Also putting your hands in your pocket will make you lose your body language which is about 55% of the message you want to deliver.

Keep your eyes towards your audience

Start your presentation with individual eye contact with your audience to break the ice and inner fear.

After getting involved in the presentation, your eye contact should reach every person in the presentation. You should stand in a position where everybody can see you and you can see everybody.

Keep your eyes moving to the right and to the left. Make every body feel like you are conducting this presentation for him only.

Never look to the ceiling or to the extreme up or to the extreme bottom (don't look to your legs).

When you give a presentation to a small audience (up to 30 persons) look to their faces to make the eye contact, look up to the nose between eyes.

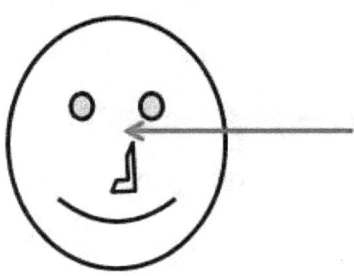

This will keep you concentrated to your presentation and you will not be distracted.

Avoid nervous habits

You should control your self if you have any nervous habits (not to distract your audience)

Repeat your important speech

When you are presenting to a large audience you need to repeat the important keywords to assure that the message reached every person in the audience.

Deal with audience characters

Any presentation includes different audience characters.

You will deal with the bold, silly, not interested and lazy people. So get ready and be patient and control your reaction to their deeds.

Grape audience attention using silence

You may use the silence as a tool to draw the audience attention. People will wait and will be curios of what you are going to say after the long silent period (about 30-60 seconds maximum).

Show your passion during presentation

You should interact with different situations during presentation showing your enthusiasm and passion.

Why the audience care about your speech if you don't show your enthusiasm or reflection about the topic you are presenting.

Use suitable language

You should use simple language that every person in the presentation should understand.

If you know multiple languages, talk to each audience with their own language.

Don't mix languages with audience that only knows single language.

Watch your pace of speech

You should speak in an understandable speed, not too fast neither too slow. Always check with your audience "is the pace of speech OK?".

Involve your audience with their names

You may speak with your audience by their names. This will make the audience focus. Don't use this step to embarrass them but to bring their minds back and to refocus on the presentation.

Encourage audience to interact.

Always try to make the presentation in two directions. Ask the audience to give you feedback. Encourage them to ask questions and thank them for asking the questions.

Question handling:

When you are asked question, Please consider the following steps:

Control the questions.

If you prefer nobody ask you during your presentation session and make interruptions for you, no problem but give the audience adequate time at the end of the presentation or each session to answer their questions.

Keep control of the questions and answers time at the end of the presentation by:

Setting a limited time like "We have only 10 minutes of questions"

On a public speech you can say "We are going to take 3 questions only!!"

After the end of Q&A period you should say "For further questions I will be at my office to answer any additional questions".

Another method to control the question is never look to the person asking the question personally (don't make eye contact) but rather look to other audience and repeat the question for the public and answer it also to the public.

If you answer the question while making a direct eye contact to the demander, it will drive you to a personal conversation. Once you answered his question he may ask you another question then another question, and then if he didn't understand he will ask another question and it will drive you to unwanted personal conversation (you will lose control).

Don't make the eye contact and always remember "For further questions I will be at my office to answer any additional questions".

Note: The previous methods used if you know that there will be difficult or silly questions that you want to avoid. But in normal conditions you should discuss with your audience and take their feedback for understanding your topic.

Don't take people questions personally and always share the question and its answer with the rest of the audience to make every body get benefit from the question.

Only reject the unethical questions like when somebody tells you in the middle of the presentation; for instance "**Your company is a group of thieves**", immediately stop him and stop the presentation until you find a solution for this situation.

Listen carefully to the meaning behind the question.

Listening is the key to respond with the right answer that the audience is waiting for.

Remember listening is different than hearing. Hearing is just to notice but listening is to understand the meaning behind the question.

Test that you understood the question.

If one of your audience asked you unclear question. Don't rapidly try to answer. Test with him that your understood the question like saying "**Did you mean …..?**). This will help you to prepare to respond with the targeted answer and not to open other issues that are no need to discuss them in the presentation.

Share questions.

To prevent repeated questions, always share questions and repeat the question to the public in order to save your time (nobody asks the question again) and to assure that the answer or the information reached everybody.

Never rate your audience questions.

You should never criticize your audience question saying for instance: "**This is a bad question**" or "**How you asked a question like that?**". The audience is here to learn from you. They should ask and ask any question. If you criticized your audience questions, they will fear from you and accordingly will not understand your presentation. It will leave a bad impression inside your audience.

Think about your response to the question.

Before you respond to audience questions think of the answer:

Is the answer will be mentioned later (no need to answer now and repeat it again later)?

Is the answer will be understood by the audience, or it is above their level of knowledge and their ability? (It will make things worse and open a channel of questions).

Will the answer direct us to another topic that will distract the audience from the main topic? (Not to go into deep information that will not benefit the presented topic and it may be discussed later personally)

Don't make up answers.

If you were asked a question that you don't know its answer. You should never make up the answer. Ethically don't do that. And don't be embarrassed. No one knows every thing, but rather say "**Actually I don't have the answer right now, I will answer you later (tomorrow for example)**".

You may make up the answer (which is wrong!!) depending on that the audience don't know the right answer,but imagine that one of the audience raised up his hand and said to you "**You are wrong and the right answer for the question is …….**".You will lose your credibility with your audience and it will be very embarrassing for you.

Check if your audience is satisfied?.

If you answered a question for one of your audience during the presentation, check with him "**Did you get the answer?**" or "Did I answer your question?" take a feedback.

Rephrase the silly questions.

One of the proven ways to avoid difficult situations is rephrasing the question. If you were asked a silly question, just think (a few seconds) then rephrase the question and make the question asks for something else related to the first question.

Example:

Imagine you are giving a lecture for the first year students in the college about electricity and its nature.

One of the students asks you (the lecturer), "If the electricity comes from electrons, dose it mean that morality comes from morons?"

You should never criticize him (not to loose him and his companions) but rephrase the question like this.

Direct your eye contact to the other audience in the hall and tell them **"One of the students asks what the electricity consists of or how the electricity comes**

from? I will explain the concept for you, ……. ". By rephrasing you will escape from the silly questions and you will not loose your audience.

Remember that you took advantage from this situation to your presentation side and you will explain the topic better.

Put your touch after audience questions.

When you are asked from your audience a question and another one of the audiences answered that question. Always put your final comment on the answer even if you will repeat it the answer again. This will make you control the speech in your hands.

Use your audience to answer.

One of the ways to overcome difficult questions is you send them back to your audience again, saying for instance "**X asks about …..? Y what do you think is the answer?**" then through it to the whole audience "**anyone knows the answer?**" May be one of the audience know the answer that you don't know.

But it could be very difficult that if he answered a wrong answer and you didn't correct him. May be one of the audience (who was silent) knows the answer and interrupt both of you and says **"The right answer is ….."** it will be very embarrassing. So be carful when you use this method.

Ask question if no one asks you a question

At the end of the presentation and before the closing you are asking the audience for questions and nobody is responding!

You may ask the question as "**There is a question people often ask me which is ……….** ". This is how you can give more information at the end of your show.

Be credible for later actions.

When you postpone an answer to one of your audience for the next few minutes or you delay answering questions (wide answer questions) to another meeting or you promise the audience to send details by email, you should be honest and do what you promised your audience to do. Because if you did not, you will lose credibility and you will lose control of your speech and the upcoming speeches.

Chapter 20: 3 Steps to Becoming the Most Charismatic Person in the Room

In her book The Charisma Myth, Olivia Fox Cabane claims that there are three components to charisma: warmth, power, and presence. Read on to learn more about each...

Charisma Key #1: Warmth. In other words, be friendly. Smile. Look approachable. Be nice. If you're an unapproachable jerk who alienates people, people are not going to consider you very charismatic.

Charisma Key #2: Power. My delivery lady is very friendly. She smiles, we make small talk whenever she delivers something, and she gives me a wave whenever I see her around. But... she's not very powerful. She's a delivery lady. She doesn't exactly have a presence that oozes of power and authority. While you don't need to be a world leader or billionaire CEO to meet this power requirement, you do need to develop an aura of power and authority. Your body language and other nonverbals are key to doing this.

Charisma Key #3: Presence. Bill Clinton is famous for his undeniable charisma. Even people who just shook his hand say that, for that split second, they felt as if it were only the two of them in existence. Everything else faded away. Bill Clinton was completely focused on them, and only them. In other words, he was fully present. Now imagine if Clinton was distracted by something else he was thinking about, off in his own little world. Or if he was simultaneously shooting off an email on his phone while meeting and greeting people. All of a sudden, he loses that awesome charisma. He has warmth and power, but without presence, he loses that charisma. So that's the final key to charisma: being fully present.

Okay, so how do you apply these three keys to charisma to your public speaking endeavors?

Let's take another look at these three keys with different ways you can use each when speaking to an audience...

Warmth. Display warmth when speaking to an audience by using humor and telling personal stories. When you open up about yourself or make yourself a little vulnerable—such as by recounting a story when you made a funny mistake (that's relevant to your speech/audience)—you allow your audience to connect with you. You can also display warmth by smiling, talking in a friendly manner, and so on.

Power. Contrary to what you might have initially thought, you don't actually need to be powerful to be charismatic. You just need to have a powerful, authoritative aura. Refer back to the first section in this book on nonverbal communication to learn how to develop a powerful, authoritative, awe-inspiring presence.

Presence. You need to be fully present and focused on your audience. Don't look at your slides. Don't look at your notes. Don't look at your feet or your hands or the exit. Focus 100 percent on your audience and be completely present. Make solid eye contact with them. Also make sure you're fully focused on the moment and not thinking about something else in the back of your mind (or else your eyes will have that glazed over look of someone who's not really there, but off in la-la land).

CHAPTER 21: The Interview Plan

1- Standard interview plan

Below is a classical TV/radio interview plan:

a. Start by presenting your guest, and the institute he represents if he represents one.

b. Announce the main subject of the interview.

c. Start with obvious basic questions to give the viewers/listeners enough basic information about the subject in question.

d. Elaborate the most essential topics and aspects of the subject.

e. If time allows, go deeper into those main topics.

f. If time allows, move to other less imperative subtopics.

g. Conclude by summing up the most important features of the subject.

2- Writing it down

Writing down your interview plan and questions is simple. However, writing it clearly enough to read it in glances during the interview is definitely tricky. To make your interview plan and question list that lucid, here's how the notes in your hand should be:

A. Clear

B. Detailed

C. Concise

A. Clear

You want to put all the topics you intend to discuss during the interview. However, you won't have the time to read details of the relevant topics. Furthermore, you need information that is set out neatly on paper in your hands during the interview. You can't look at a paper full of long sentences, and be able to catch up immediately on the question you want to ask next. And if you manage to decipher the question in such chaos, you'll most probably ramble it out rather than ask it properly. Your paper is messed up, which means the layout of your questions will be messed up as well. You have to help your brain get the thoughts organised, help your mind stay clear and focused. This will help you relax, feel confident, and be in control throughout your show.

And the best way to do this is to state the topic in the title, then mention the main points that should be discussed about that topic (as shown in the coming paragraph 3: 'Plan Layout').

B. Detailed

You have to mention the topics to be discussed, and note, next to each topic, important details you don't want to forget, such as names, dates, and locations. Beneath the topic, mention the sub-topic to be discussed and a few necessary details within the sub-topic as well (as shown in the coming paragraph 3: 'Plan Layout').

C. Concise

By concise we mean that you shouldn't write anything that you won't have time to read, yet at the same time, shouldn't leave out any details that you definitely should remember. You mention the point to discuss, and then note any important names, dates, locations to remember. You don't need to write down the whole question as if you're going to read it out word for word. However, you can do this if it is a complicated question, and you therefore feel the need to have it written down for you to be able to remember it and ask it properly. This is mostly necessary in political interviews where you need to pose problematic questions. Remember that such a question has to be clear as well. So if you need to elaborate a little, and formulate the whole question as it will be asked during the interview, do it.

3. Plan Layout

Example plan: Interview with a singer about a new album:

Guest name: Singer X

Topic 1. New Album: 'Album name'.

A. The writers of the songs

B. The music composers

C. Release date

D. ...etc.

Topic 2. Tournament (starting date 20/12/2011):

A. Cities (Berlin, California, Paris.)

B. Expectations

C. Event organisers

D. ...etc.

This layout will allow you to check your plan at a glance. You might think that this plan has only the very basics, and that you don't need to write that down in order to remember it. The most powerful and famous interviewers of our time, when asked about the ultimate advice they can give, all say: having at hand well-written interview notes and questions. This is because they have experienced it, and they know that you can never control what might happen during a live aired interview. The best way to be in control and prepared for any unexpected event is to have all your notes and researched information written down properly, clearly, and concisely. Whenever you feel the need for more details to remember your question, state them, and state the whole question if you feel you need it. Do whatever makes you feel well prepared and makes you feel confident about and ready for the interview. It's understandable, especially at the beginning of your career as a TV/radio presenter, if you feel more relaxed and confident if you have the whole question written down. As you get more experience and gain more confidence, you'll find yourself gradually losing this habit.

4- Controlling the interview flow

1- Listen to the answers. It's a difficult balance, listening while still preparing what question to ask next, but it's important. Listening and responding appropriately to your subject creates rapport.

2- Ask any unscripted question that arises naturally from a response. Questions that flow out of the conversation will get better answers than queries that seem canned or come out of nowhere.

3- Use your scripted question order only as a guideline. Skip around if one of your questions seems more appropriate when asked earlier or later in the interview.

4- Announce drastic changes in the subject. Sometimes it's unavoidable that further questions require a 180° turn from what you've already been discussing. Letting the guest know that you're shifting focus makes it less awkward when you present your new query. And you'll have a more harmonious conversation as a result.

5- Mention a personal fact or experience if it's pertinent. An interview can sound like an interrogation if the interviewer never offers any personal information, such as discussing a song you both liked. Just remember to keep it brief and go back on track to your main subject.

6- Discuss, don't interrogate.

7- Announce the final question. Knowing it's the end of the interview will usually relax the subject, and the guest might add some thoughts to sum up the topic.

Chapter 22: The Power of Charm

Imagine you're a member of the audience and you are excited to hear the speaker. After waiting for hours, the MC finally appeared and introduced the man of the hour. Then the awaited person makes himself visible breaking through the curtains dressed in his rugged attire. Would you believe that he is the person with all that wisdom to share?

Unless you're Steve Jobs, dressing up is very important no matter how small or large the numbers of your audience are. Your general facade reflects your seriousness of the event and shows that you're not going to waste their time. If the event is formal, then dress appropriately.

Put on clothes that make you confident and comfortable. It will not only raise the level of your positivity, it will also directly influence the perception of the viewers. While grooming is already evident that it increases a person's likability, studies further confirm the impact of it.

Make yourself charming by styling your hair and dressing up appropriately. Make yourself look clean. The more attractive you become, the more influential you will be.

And when you are finally in the spotlight, smile! But of course, put that grin aside if what you are about to deliver is a eulogy (unless you are confident the bereaved will appreciate hearing a rather humorous true story about the deceased). Smiling is one of the excellent ways to establish rapport. It radiates poise and positivity. An experiment involving 169 participants who were asked to complete a series of stress-inducing activities led to a fascinating finding. The group who were instructed to smile while performing the tasks had significantly reduced heart rates compared to the control group.

While already-popular personalities can pull off such acts dressing in their shirts and jeans, bear in mind that you are still trying to sell something and that is yourself. Note that your first impression is crucial, but it will not dictate the result. Obviously, your message should be valued over appearance.

Again, to dominate your audience, you first need to build your rapport. First impressions are essential to winning the audience. Groom your hair, trim your facial hair (for men), put on your best-fitting clothes, and don't forget to smile.

Chapter 23: Self Confidence: The Foundation of Professional Speakers

Speakers have their own styles in delivering their message. Some use humor, while others use a more formal or challenging approach. But one thing that notable speakers have in common is that they are able to influence their listeners. Whether the audience develops an interest in the topic that was spoken about or learns a new skill, one thing is certain the speakers had an impact on the listeners. This is achieved because of one key trait: self confidence.

When you stand in front of an audience, you are there to serve a purpose. The first chapter of this book listed the different reasons why speeches are made. So whether you are speaking to persuade, inspire, or teach, your audience needs to be receptive to the information you are sharing. One of the elements they look at when listening to speeches is how confident the speakers are. This will give then an indication of your credibility. Your self confidence will help them decide, whether consciously or subconsciously, that you are worth listening to.

While some people seem to naturally possess this trait, there are those who find it difficult to deal with stage fright or public speaking anxiety. Because of this, even if they are experts in the field they are speaking about, their message is not delivered with the confidence it requires to have a positive impact.

The great news though is that it is something that almost anyone can develop. All it takes is a conscious effort to remain calm and confident. With a lot of practice, you can start exuding self confidence in all of your speaking engagements. Here are some tips on how you can develop this trait:

Self confidence comes from knowing that you have the knowledge and ability necessary to successfully deliver the message. Having a well researched and prepared speech can help you feel confident about standing in front of an audience.

Focus on what you want to happen rather than on the things you want to prevent from happening. For example, visualize yourself being able to entertain the audience rather than picturing yourself giving a boring speech.

Being nervous does not mean that you are not confident. Expect to feel a little jittery at the beginning. There is no need to eliminate these jitters as it is completely natural to be nervous at first. Simply convert these jitters into positive energy to deliver a more engaging speech

Don't forget to breathe. You would be surprised at how calming it is to take in some air when you find yourself feeling anxious.

Stage fright is often caused by the thought of being at the center of everyone's attention. Simply thinking about having dozens of eyes focused on you is enough to give you an anxiety attack. The best way to get over this is to get to meet some of your audience before your speech. This can help you relax as you get a better insight of the people you will be speaking to. Your audience will also get to know you ahead of time so they would be more open to the message you will be relaying.

While you could use other speakers as an inspiration, resist the urge to compare yourself with them. Each speaker has their own strengths and this is what you need to focus on. Consider what you are able to bring to the table and do not think about how you fare compared to other experts.

Practice. It may seem like a cliché but practicing will definitely help you become more familiar with what you will be delivering. The more comfortable you are with your speech, the more confident you will be on the actual day of your speaking engagement.

Visit the venue if possible. Part of the anxiety or nervousness that you feel is due to unfamiliar surroundings. Remove this factor by simply seeing where you will be speaking. It is the same as home court advantage for sports teams. By orienting yourself with the location, you can already plan ahead of time how you can choreograph your speech. You can also see any possible roadblocks or challenges so you can make the necessary adjustments ahead of time.

Pay special attention to your appearance. Shallow as it may sound to some, it is easier to feel extra confident if you know that you look good. You can use this to your advantage by dressing appropriately so you do not feel awkward in front of everybody.

Confidence is different from arrogance. It will be beneficial for you to remember this. Be confident but not smug. Treat your listeners with respect. They, in return, will accord you with the same treatment.

Self confidence is a reflection of how competent and comfortable you feel being in front of everybody else. Focus on the elements that will help you feel that you are the best person to make the speech and your audience will feel and appreciate the confidence you will be exuding.

Conclusion

As you can see from the chapters of this book, there is a lot of work involved in giving adequate and successful speeches. Your preparation, the way you look and the way that you present your speech all have a bearing on how listeners perceive your skills to be. What you need to do is prepare your speech, practice it to perfection and be aware of the people that you are speaking to.

I have heard some great speeches from inexperienced speakers because they took the time to prepare for that speech. They were not the most eloquent of speakers but what saved the day was that they knew their subjects and were able to give a very powerful argument in favor of their subject.

It helps that you know a lot about the speech. It helps that you know which side you are on and can argue effectively to win people over. Once you learn all of these techniques, you will no longer be nervous as a public speaker and will be able to address larger audiences with much more confidence.

Thank you and good luck!

www.ingramcontent.com/pod-product-compliance
Lightning Source LLC
Chambersburg PA
CBHW072009070526
44583CB00015B/1398